The Professional Caterer Series

Volume 1

Pastry Hors d'œuvres - Mini-Sandwiches Canapés - Assorted Snacks - Hot Hors d'œuvres Cold Brochettes - Centerpieces for Buffets

Denis Ruffel

assisted by

Roland Bilheux and Alain Escoffier

under the direction of
Pierre Michalet

Translated by Anne Sterling

A copublication of
CICEM (Compagnie Internationale
de Consultation *Education* et *Media*)
Paris

and

**Van Nostrand Reinhold
New York**

Contents

About the Translators

Anne Sterling began her cooking career by catering at Kalamazoo College in Michigan, where she majored in French. In 1980, she earned the Grand Diplôme from La Varenne Ecole de Cuisine in Paris, and followed her formal training with two years of apprenticeships, including a period with Denis Ruffel, author of this series. After cooking on a luxury barge in Burgundy, she returned to the U.S., where she worked as a menu consultant, catering chef and organizer of gastronomic trips to France. In 1986, she returned to Paris to take the position of director of La Varenne. She is presently writing, lecturing and developing a program of delicious and healthy menus for babies, enjoyed by her young daughter Elizabeth.

Anne Sterling was assisted by Martha Holmberg, who worked for several years as an editor before changing careers to enter the cooking field in 1984. After working as a chef and caterer in the U.S., she came to Paris in 1988, where she earned the Grand Diplôme from La Varenne and continues freelance work as a cookbook editor and private caterer.

Introduction to the 7 Families of

The Caterer's Repertoire of Individual Hors d'œuvres for Buffets and Receptions

Just as the musical scale has seven notes, the professional caterer's repertoire includes seven families of hors d'œuvres to serve for buffets or receptions or sell in specialty food shops.

By organizing these preparations in seven families, selections can be made from each family for a well-rounded assortment, or you can create menus from a few of the families.

1. Pastry Hors d'œuvres

This assortment of hors d'œuvres is perfect served with cocktails or champagne before a reception or a dinner.

They are prepared with a base made of pastry (puff pastry, pie pastry) or bread (white bread, pizza dough).

They keep very well and are easy to serve, therefore they are a good choice to offer at a stand-up buffet.

4. "Les Mignonnettes" (Assorted Snacks)

A little out of the ordinary, these tasty bite-sized creations add a festive touch to any selection of hors d'œuvres.

Since their preparation overall is somewhat lengthy, and in some cases needs special handling at the last minute, they are not as common at receptions as the other hors d'œuvres presented here.

5. Hot Hors d'œuvres

These hors d'œuvres are especially popular at evening buffets and during cold weather.

As they are usually served hot, they require a great deal of organization at the time of service.

Served with other hot refreshments, they can round out the assortment of a dinner buffet.

"The Professional Caterer" (Volume 1)

2. Mini Sandwiches

The freshness and variety of these sandwiches are always popular with younger groups. They would therefore be a good choice for receptions where children will be present or a get together after a sporting event.

3. Canapés

Canapés are subtle and complex and are appreciated on more sophisticated occasions. Since they are made with such a vast selection of ingredients, the caterer must be very organized in order to produce a variety of canapés. The final aspic glaze requires that these canapés be prepared in two steps and then kept chilled until ready to serve. The wide variety of colors, tastes, and price make this family an especially important one for the caterer.

6. Centerpieces for Buffets

These stunning centerpieces add color and dimension to any buffet. Their fresh appearance and taste is always a pleasure for the customers. They are appropriate for all occasions, in any season.

Even though they are easy to assemble, the final result depends on the artistic flair of the caterer (choice of colors, ingredients).

7. Cold Brochettes

These colorful brochettes with their variety of ingredients and glazes are as delicious as they are beautiful.

Their preparation is somewhat lengthy, therefore these brochettes are usually served for more important occasions when they can be fully appreciated.

Chapter 1
Pastry Hors d'œuvres

~~~~~~~~~~~~~~~~

In the caterer's repertoire, pastry hors d'œuvres are the most convenient and easy to pass among guests at a reception.

These bite-size, easily prepared hors d'œuvres therefore are ideal to serve:

- as the main item at a cocktail reception,
- to round out the selection on a hot or cold buffet,
- to accompany certain dishes during a meal,
- as snacks throughout the day.

These hors d'œuvres taste best when served warm.

They require the skills of a pastry chef and are particularly delicious when they are well-prepared. They are not expensive to make and they store very well and therefore are practical to make ahead when the kitchen is less busy for sale at a future date. In a specialty shop a small assortment can be displayed in a disposable container or they can be arranged on a platter, leaving the customer to choose the variety and number he needs. The pastry hors d'œuvres are always sold by weight. They are popular items that are sure to sell.

General Advice

There are many techniques in this chapter that are important for achieving pastry that is delicate, crispy and evenly formed. Among the helpful hints to remember are the following:

1. For all pastry, brush away excess flour from the rolled out sheet of dough before shaping. This is most efficiently accomplished with a large soft-bristled brush which can also be used to brush flour off the work surface. If flour is not brushed off the pastry, the glaze will not adhere properly, and in the case of puff pastry, excess flour between the layers will prevent it from rising properly.

2. After pastries are shaped with a knife or pastry cutter, best results will be achieved if each piece is turned over onto the baking sheet for the following reasons: the side facing the work surface is smoother than the side that has been rolled out; the cutter makes a clean cut when it makes contact with the work surface so by reversing the pastry, this side is up; in the case of puff pastry, the action of pressing down with the cutter is reversed when the piece of dough is flipped so that the layers are more likely to rise higher.

3. The shaped pastries are placed on a baking sheet that has been moistened either with a mister (atomizer) or pastry brush dipped in water. This water on the baking sheet sticks the pastry in place and therefore helps prevent shrinkage during cooking.

4. After cutting bite-size puff pastry shapes, they are more likely to rise evenly if four tiny holes are pricked in an even north-south-east-west pattern with the tip of a paring knife or the point of a skewer. These "air vents" allow a small amount of the trapped steam to escape which helps avoid lopsided pastry. Be sure to prick the holes after the pastry is glazed as the egg glaze will fill up the holes.

5. Pastry is often glazed twice, which ensures a richer golden color and an even-textured surface with no streaks. The pastries may be glazed once after shaping and again just before baking.

6. Cutting shapes from pastry creates lots of trimmings. In the case of puff pastry, the excess pastry can be incorporated in a neat flat layer before the sixth turn. This "puff pastry plus trimmings" may not rise quite as high as puff pastry with no trimmings, but will be just as delicate and light and enables the caterer to avoid waste. Use only trimmings that have not been previously brushed with egg glaze.

The Five Families of Pastry Hors d'œuvres

These 28 hors d'œuvres are divided into five families according to the base and fillings.

The first three families are made with puff pastry, but are assembled differently.

The fourth family includes hors d'œuvres made with three different crusts.

The fifth is made with pie pastry baked in a small mold with a custard and different fillings.

A - Simple Puff Pastry Hors d'œuvres

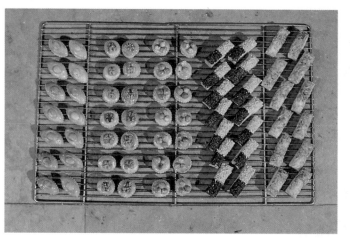

These are made in different shapes with a base of puff pastry and garnished with nuts, seeds or cheese. After they are baked, they are ready to serve.

B - Filled Puff Pastry Hors d'œuvres

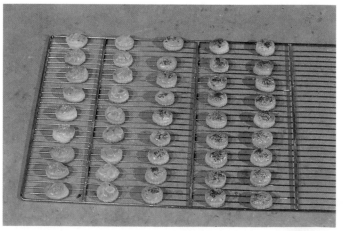

After these rounds of puff pastry are baked, they are split open and filled with a sauce usually made with cheese. The pastry and sauce can be made ahead and the hors d'œuvres filled at the last minute.

C - Combination Puff Pastry Hors d'œuvres

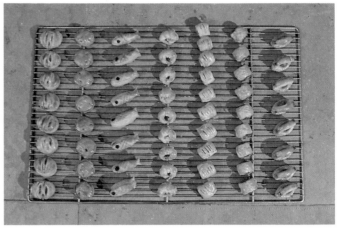

These hors d'œuvres are different in that they are filled before they are baked, allowing the pastry to absorb the flavor of the filling. They are assembled two ways: placing the filling between two layers of pastry or rolling the pastry around filling and cutting into pieces.

D - Pizzas, "Gougères" and "Croque-monsieurs"

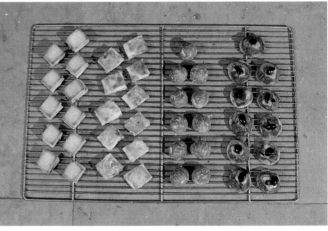

This family includes three different doughs: pizza dough for the pizza, cream puff dough for the "gougères" and white bread dough for the "croque-monsieurs".

E - Mini-Tartelettes

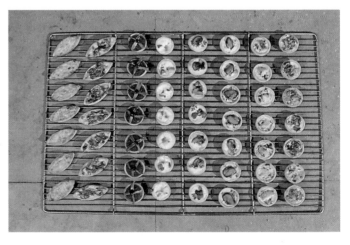

These hors d'œuvres are made in round and barquette (boat-shaped) molds using a basic pie pastry or sturdier "pâté pastry" as a base. The filling consists of vegetables, cheese or seafood mixed with a light custard. After they are filled, they are baked in the oven.

A - Simple Puff Pastry Hors d'œuvres

Since the preparation of these hors d'œuvres creates a certain number of trimmings from the pastry, you can use the trimmings to incorporate during the sixth "turn" in a future batch of puff pastry (see p. 8). The pastry should be rolled out to no thinner than 3mm (1/8in).

The pastry needs to rest and chill before being cut out to avoid shrinkage during baking. Pay particular attention to the neatness and uniformity of the pieces. Carefully brush on an egg glaze that will make them shiny and golden.

Freezing

Once cut into shapes, these small pastries can be made in sizeable batches and frozen in a raw state, which is not only profitable for the caterer, but offers a large assortment to the customer. They can be taken from the freezer, glazed and baked immediately.

Baking

Bake the small pastries in a medium high oven (210C (400F)) so that they will not dry out. Do not bake pastries of different sizes on the same baking sheet to insure even cooking.

Storage

It is preferable to store these pastries at room temperature. For best results however, they should be baked fresh daily.

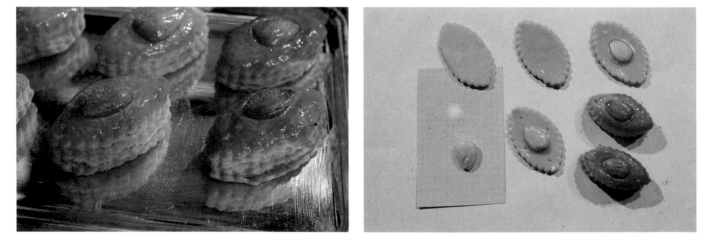

No. 1 Almond Hors d'œuvres

Equipment

Baking sheet, pastry brush, brush, rolling pin, fluted oval 7.5cm (3in) pastry cutter.

Ingredients

Puff pastry with trimmings, blanched almonds, egg glaze, salt.

Procedure

Roll out a sheet of puff pastry 3mm (1/8in) thick. Cut out the shapes with the cutter.

Turn the pieces over and place them on a moistened baking sheet.

Brush on two coats of egg glaze. Place a blanched almond in the center and press on it gently with your thumb to stick it to the pastry.

Glaze the almond and sprinkle with salt.

Prick the pastry to help it rise evenly.

No. 2 Walnut Hors d'œuvres

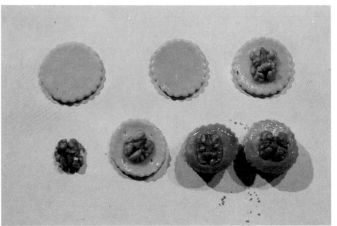

Equipment

Baking sheet, pastry brush, brush, round fluted 5cm (2in) pastry cutter, rolling pin.

Ingredients

Puff pastry with trimmings, walnut halves, egg glaze.

Procedure

Roll out a sheet of puff pastry 3mm (1/8in) thick. Cut out the shapes with the cutter.

Turn the pieces over and place them on a moistened baking sheet.

Brush on two coats of egg glaze. Place a walnut half in the center and press on it gently with your thumb to stick it to the pastry, taking care not to break the nut. Do not glaze or salt the walnut, as this would interfere with the look and the taste.

Prick the pastry to help it rise evenly.

No. 3 Hazelnut Hors d'œuvres

Equipment

Baking sheet, pastry brush, round fluted 5cm (2in) pastry cutter, rolling pin, brush.

Ingredients

Puff pastry with trimmings, hazelnuts, egg glaze, salt.

Procedure

Roll out a sheet of puff pastry 3mm (1/8in) thick. Cut out the shapes with the cutter.

Turn the pieces over and place them on a moistened baking sheet.

Brush on two coats of egg glaze. Place three hazelnuts in the center and press gently with your thumb to stick them to the pastry. Glaze the hazelnuts and sprinkle with salt.

Prick the pastry to help it rise evenly.

No. 4 Poppy Seed and Sesame Seed Matchsticks

Brush egg glaze on one half of the band and place the ruler on the other half. Cover the glazed half with sesame seeds.

Equipment

Baking sheet, rolling pin, pastry brush, brush, ruler, pastry wheel, chef's knife, parchment paper, cardboard.

Now place the ruler on top of the sesame seeds along the center line, glaze the other half and cover with poppy seeds.

Place a sheet of parchment paper on top of the band, and press the seeds down gently with the rolling pin.

Procedure

Roll out a sheet of puff pastry to 3mm (1/8in). Cut bands of pastry 9cm (3 1/2in) wide and place them

Brush away excess seeds.

Chill before cutting into strips.

Ingredients

Puff pastry with trimmings, egg glaze, poppy seeds, sesame seeds

on a sheet of parchment paper. Mark the middle of each band with a ruler.

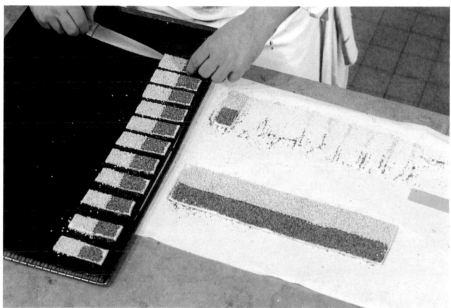

Cut a rectangular pattern from a piece of thin cardboard 2.5cm × 9cm (1in × 3 1/2in). Cut the chilled bands using the cardboard strip as a guide so that all the pieces are the same size which is important for the final presentation.

Place the matchsticks on a moistened baking sheet leaving enough space in between so that they will bake evenly.

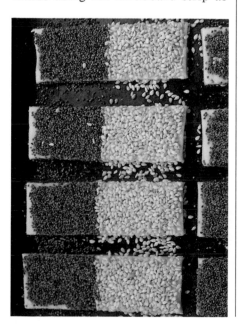

No. 5 Cheese Matchsticks

Season lightly with salt, pepper and paprika.

Place a sheet of parchment paper on top of the band and press down lightly with the rolling pin to stick the cheese to the glaze.

Chill before cutting into strips.

Make a rectangular pattern from a piece of cardboard 2.5cm × 9cm (1in × 3 1/2in). Cut the band into even strips using the cardboard pattern as a guide.

Place the matchsticks on a moistened baking sheet, leaving space between them so they bake evenly.

Equipment

Baking sheet, rolling pin, pastry brush, brush, ruler, pastry wheel, chef's knife, parchment paper, cardboard.

Ingredients

Puff pastry with trimmings, grated swiss cheese, salt, pepper, paprika.

Procedure

Roll out a sheet of puff pastry to 3mm (1/8in). Cut into 9cm (3 1/2in) bands and place them on a sheet of parchment paper.

Apply one coat of egg glaze to the whole band. Cover the glazed pastry with a generous layer of grated swiss cheese.

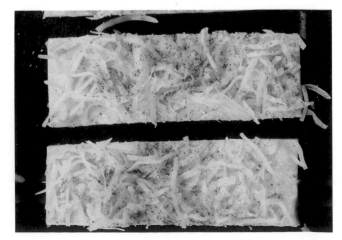

B - Filled Hors d'œuvres

General Advice

For these hors d'œuvres, you can use puff pastry with trimmings incorporated during the sixth turn (see p. 8). The pastry should be rolled out to no thinner than 3mm (1/8in). Always allow the pastry to rest as required.

Chill the pastry before baking. Pay attention to the neatness and uniformity of the shapes.

Freezing

These small hors d'œuvres can be successfully frozen in a raw state, whether they are partially or completely assembled.

Baking

Do not overbake these pastries, which destroys their delicate flavor and makes them more difficult to split evenly for filling.

Split the pastries while they are still warm.

Filling

The baked pastries should be cool before they are filled with the sauce.

Fill the pastries to the rim with a pastry bag fitted with a small tip. Avoid filling them too full as they will overflow when they are reheated, which will ruin their appearance.

Storage

Once they are filled, these hors-d'œuvre with their delicate sauces should be carefully stored until ready to reheat.

No. 6 Parmesan-filled Hors d'œuvres

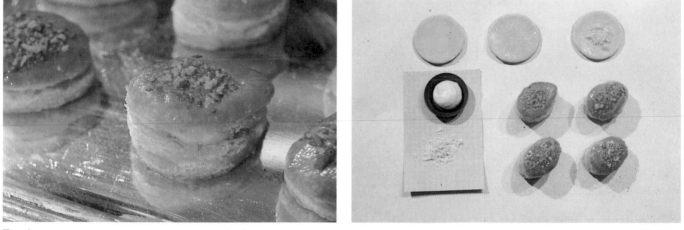

Equipment

Baking sheet, rolling pin, brush, pastry brush, plain round 5cm (2in) pastry cutter, pastry bag and small plain tip.

Ingredients

Puff pastry with trimmings, egg

glaze, grated parmesan cheese, parmesan sauce.

Procedure

Roll out a sheet of puff pastry to 3mm (1/8in). Cut out the shapes with the cutter. Turn the pieces over and place them on a moistened baking sheet. Brush with two coats of egg glaze. Prick the pastry to help it rise evenly. Place some grated parmesan in the center of each shape. Chill for at least 1 hour.

Bake at 210C (400F) for about 15 minutes.

Split open the warm shapes using a paring knife.

Filling : Using the pastry bag fit-

ted with a small plain tip, fill the shapes with parmesan sauce and replace the lids.

Parmesan Sauce

1/2L (2 cups) milk, 60g (2oz) butter, 2 eggs, 40g (1 1/2 oz) corn starch, 125g (4oz) grated parmesan or swiss cheese, salt, pepper, grated nutmeg.

No. 7 Sliced Almond Hors d'œuvres

Equipment

Baking sheet, rolling pin, brush, pastry brush, knife, round fluted 5cm (2in) pastry cutter, pastry bag and small plain tip.

Ingredients

Puff pastry with trimmings, egg glaze, sliced almonds, roquefort cream, salt.

Procedure

Roll out a sheet of puff pastry to 3mm (1/8in). Cut out the shapes with the cutter, turn them over and place on a moistened baking sheet.

Coat the shapes twice with egg glaze and prick the pastry to help it rise evenly.

Place three sliced almonds in the center of each round. Glaze and salt the almonds. Chill for at least 1 hour before baking.

Baking

Bake at 210C (400F) for 15-20 minutes. Split the warm shapes using a paring knife and leave to cool.

Roquefort Cream

45g (1 1/2oz) roquefort cheese, 100g (3 1/2oz) parmesan sauce.

Blend until smooth with a whisk.

Filling

Using the pastry bag fitted with a small plain tip, fill the shapes with the roquefort cream and replace the lids.

No. 8 Cumin-Munster Hors d'œuvres

Equipment

Baking sheet, rolling pin, brush, pastry brush, fluted round 5cm (2in) pastry cutter, pastry bag fitted with a small plain tip.

Ingredients

Puff pastry with trimmings, egg glaze, cumin seeds, munster cream

Procedure

Roll out a sheet of puff pastry to 3mm (1/8in). Cut out the shapes with the 5cm (2in) cutter. Turn the shapes over and place them on a moistened baking sheet.

Coat the shapes twice with egg glaze and prick the pastry to help it

rise evenly. Sprinkle with a few cumin seeds. Leave to chill.

Bake at 210C (400F) about 15 minutes. Split the warm shapes using a paring knife.

Munster Cream

100g (3 1/2oz) munster cheese,

100g (3 1/2oz) fromage frais or cottage cheese passed through a fine sieve.

Remove the rind from the munster then pass it through a fine sieve. Stir well with the "fromage frais".

No. 9 Paprika Hors d'œuvres

Equipment

Baking sheet, rolling pin, brush, pastry brush, round fluted 5cm (2in) pastry cutter, pastry bag fitted with a plain small tip.

Ingredients

Puff pastry with trimmings, egg glaze, paprika, paprika cream.

Procedure

Roll out a sheet of puff pastry to 3mm (1/8in). Cut out the shapes with the 5cm (2in) cutter.

Turn over the pieces and place them on a moistened baking sheet.

Brush on two coats of egg glaze and prick the pastry to help it rise evenly. Sprinkle with paprika. Chill at least 1 hour.

Baking

Bake at 210C (400F) for about 15 minutes.

Split the warm shapes using a paring knife.

Paprika Cream

200g (7oz) "fromage frais" or cottage cheese, 1 teaspoon heavy cream, paprika.

Blend all ingredients with a whisk until smooth.

Filling

Using a pastry bag fitted with a small tip, fill the shapes with the paprika cream and replace the lids.

No. 10 Poppyseed Hors d'œuvres

Equipment

Baking sheet, rolling pin, brush, pastry brush, knife, round fluted 5cm (2in) pastry cutter, pastry bag fitted with a small plain tip.

Ingredients

Puff pastry with trimmings, egg glaze, poppy seeds, herb cream.

Procedure

Roll out a sheet of puff pastry to 3mm (1/8in). Cut out the shapes with the pastry cutter, turn them over and place them on a moistened baking sheet. Brush with two coats of egg glaze and prick with a paring knife. Sprinkle the poppy seeds on top and chill about 1 hour.

Baking

Bake at 210C (400F) about 15 minutes. Split the warm shapes using a paring knife.

Herb Cream

200g (7oz) fromage frais or cottage cheese, 1 teaspoon heavy cream, 2 tablespoons finely chopped fresh herbs (chervil, tarragon, chives).

Filling

Blend all ingredients with a whisk and adjust seasoning. Using the pastry bag fitted with a small plain tip, fill the shapes with the herb cream and replace the lids.

C - Combination Hors d'œuvres
No. 11 Pâté Hors d'œuvres

Equipment

Baking sheet, rolling pin, brush, roller-docker, plain round 4cm (1 3/4in) and 5cm (2in) pastry cutters, pastry brush, lattice cutter, pastry wheel, parchment paper.

Ingredients

Puff pastry with trimmings, egg glaze, pâté stuffing.

Pâté Stuffing

500g (1lb) veal, 500g (1lb) pork, 1 egg, 2 shallots chopped, 45g (1 1/2oz) chopped parsley, 5cl (1/4 cup) white wine, 2.5cl (1/8 cup) cognac, salt, pepper, mixed spices.

Beat all ingredients together until thoroughly combined. Roll into small balls as shown. Freeze.

Procedure

Roll out a sheet of puff pastry 1.5mm (1/16in) thick. Place it on a sheet of parchment paper and divide into two. Dip the top of the larger pastry cutter in flour and

lightly mark one half of the pastry in staggered rows to indicate the placement of the filling. Brush the pastry with egg glaze then prick with the roller-docker. In the center of each marked circle, place 1 ball of frozen stuffing.

Cut a lattice into the second half of the pastry using a lattice cutter and lay this second sheet over the

stuffing. Press the pastry down around the stuffing with the brush.

Dip the top of the smaller cutter in flour and seal the stuffed shapes by pressing gently. Chill to set. Cut out the shapes using the larger cutter. Remove the trimmings.

Place the hors d'œuvres on a moistened baking sheet. Brush with egg glaze and prick the pastry to help it rise evenly. Chill one hour before cooking. Bake at 210C (400F) about 20 minutes. Transfer to a rack as soon as they are cooked.

No. 12 Chorizo Hors d'œuvres

Equipment

Baking sheet, rolling pin, brush, roller-docker, plain round 4cm (1 3/4in) and 5cm (2in) pastry cutters, pastry brush, parchment paper, paring knife.

Ingredients

Puff pastry with trimmings, egg glaze, chorizo or other flavorful sausage.

Procedure

Chill the chorizo, peel off the skin and cut into 6mm (1/4in) slices. Roll out a sheet of puff pastry to 1.5mm (1/16in) and place it on a sheet of parchment paper. Cut the pastry in two.

Dip the top of the larger cutter in flour and mark circles on one half of the dough in staggered rows. Brush the pastry with egg glaze and score with the roller-docker.

Filling

Lay one slice of chorizo in the center of each marked circle. Turn over the second half of pastry and lay on top. Press the pastry down around the chorizo with the brush.

Dip the top of the smaller cutter in flour and seal the pastry by pressing lightly.

Chill to set.

Assembly

Cut out the hors d'œuvres with the larger cutter. Remove the trimmings. Place the hors d'œuvres on a moistened baking sheet, brush with egg glaze and prick the pastry to help it rise evenly. Chill at least 1 hour before cooking.

Baking

Bake at 210C (400F) about 18 minutes. Transfer to a rack to cool.

No. 13 Anchovy Hors d'œuvres

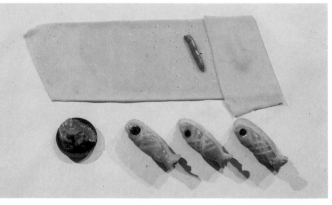

Equipment

Baking sheet, rolling pin, paring knife, brush, pastry brush, roller-docker, pastry bag fitted with small plain tip, fish-shaped pastry cutter, parchment paper.

Ingredients

Puff pastry with trimmings, egg glaze, anchovy cream, currants.

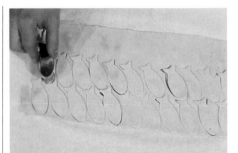

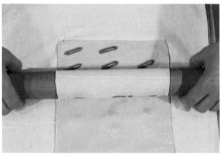

Procedure

Roll out a sheet of puff pastry to 1.5mm (1/16in). Place it on a sheet of parchment paper and cut it into two pieces. Dip the top of the cutter in flour and mark one half of the pastry with staggered rows of fishes. Brush the pastry with egg glaze and score with the roller-docker.

Anchovy Cream

250g (1/2lb) drained anchovy fillets, 45g (1 1/2oz) butter.
Blend until smooth.

Filling

Using the pastry bag and small tip, pipe a line of anchovy cream down the center of each marked fish, leaving a border at the head and tail ends. Turn over the second half of the pastry and lay on top. Press the pastry down around the cream with the brush.
Chill to set.

Assembly

Cut out the hors d'œuvres using the fish-shaped cutter. Remove the trimmings. Lay the hors d'œuvres on a moistened baking sheet, brush with egg glaze and score with a paring knife. Place a currant on each fish to look like an eye. Lightly score in lines with a paring knife.

Baking

Bake at 210C (400F) about 15 minutes. Transfer to a rack to cool.

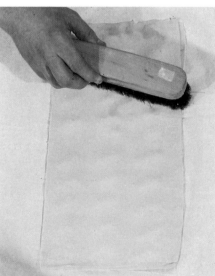

No. 14 Ham Crescents

Procedure

Roll out a sheet of puff pastry to 1.5mm (1/16in) and place on a sheet of parchment paper. Cut the sheet of dough into 10cm (4in) wide bands. For large quantities, lightly flour the sheets and lay three on top of each other. Cut the bands into triangles with 7.5cm (3in) base and 10cm (4in) sides. Lay out the triangles in rows.

Filling

Lay a small strip of ham on the base of each triangle. Dot the three corners with egg glaze. Roll up the crescents and press lightly to seal the two points together. Place on a moistened baking sheet. Brush

with one coat of egg glaze then chill at least one hour. Brush with a second coat of egg glaze.

Baking

Bake at 210C (400F) for 15 minutes. Immediately remove the pastries to a cooling rack.

Equipment

Baking sheet, rolling pin, paring knife, brush, pastry brush, parchment paper.

Ingredients

Puff pastry with trimmings, egg glaze, ham.

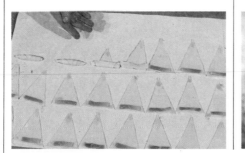

No. 15 Cocktail Sausage Hors d'œuvres

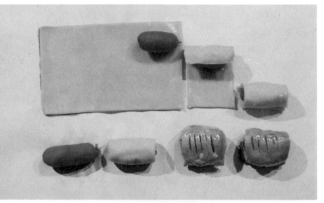

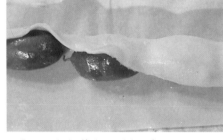

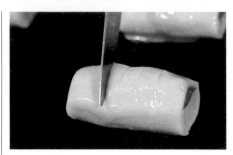

Equipment

Baking sheet, rolling pin, paring knife, brush, pastry brush, pastry wheel, parchment paper.

Ingredients

Puff pastry and trimmings, egg glaze, cocktail sausages.

Procedure

Roll out a sheet of puff pastry to

1.5mm (1/16in) and lay it on a sheet of parchment paper. Brush a 10cm (4in) wide band with egg glaze.

Filling

Place the cocktail sausages in links on the dough then roll it up to completely wrap them (the dough will wrap around about 1 1/2 times). Using the pastry wheel, cut the dough, then press lightly to seal. Chill to set.

Assembly

Using a chef's knife, cut the pastry into individual links. Lay them on a moistened baking sheet, brush with egg glaze and score with the paring knife. Leave to rest in the refrigerator at least 1 hour.

Baking

Bake at 210C (400F) for about 20 minutes. Immediately transfer to a cooling rack.

No. 16 "Chipolatas" Hors d'œuvres

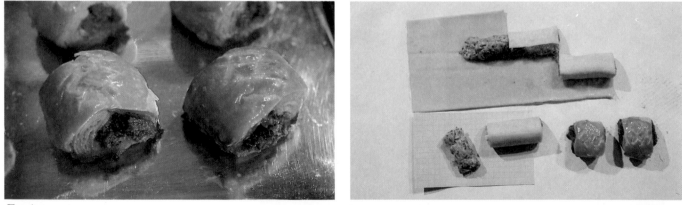

Equipment

Baking sheet, rolling pin, brush, pastry brush, chef's knife, pastry bag fitted with a large tip, parchment paper, triangular spatula.

Ingredients

Puff pastry, egg glaze, sausage meat.

Procedure

Roll out a sheet of puff pastry to 1.5mm (1/16in) and lay it on a

sheet of parchment paper. Pipe out long rolls of sausage meat onto a tray using the pastry bag and large

tip. Chill in the freezer to set. Lift the sausage rolls off the tray using a triangular spatula.

Sausage Meat

1 kg (2lb) sausage meat, 1 egg, 2 shallots, 45g (1 1/2oz) chopped parsley, 5cl (1/4 cup) white wine, 2.5cl (1/8 cup) cognac, salt, pepper, mixed spices.

Filling

Brush a 10 cm wide band of egg glaze on the dough. Lay the roll of sausage meat on the dough and roll it up in pastry (the dough will wrap around about 1 1/2 times). Seal the seam by pressing lightly. Chill to set.

Assembly

Slice the rolls into 3.5cm (1 1/2in) pieces. Place them on a moistened baking sheet. Brush with egg glaze and score in a diamond pattern with a paring knife. Leave to rest in the refrigerator at least 1 hour.

Baking

Bake at 210C (400F) for about 20 minutes. Immediately transfer to a cooling rack.

No. 17 Stuffed Olive Hors d'œuvres

Ingredients

Puff pastry with trimmings, egg glaze, stuffed olives.

Procedure

Roll out a sheet of puff pastry to 1.5mm (1/16in) and lay it on a sheet of parchment paper. Cut out shapes with the pastry cutter. Turn the shapes over and lay them on a moistened baking sheet. Brush with two coats of egg glaze.

Equipment

Baking sheet, rolling pin, brush, pastry brush, chef's knife, oval fluted 7.5cm (3in) pastry cutter, parchment paper.

Filling

Place a stuffed olive in the center of each oval with the filling side to side. Cut 7.5cm × 1.5cm (3in × 1/2in) strips from the remaining dough. Lay the strips of dough on the ovals lengthwise, allowing the stuffing in the olives to show.

Brush the hors d'œuvres with egg glaze and prick once on the edges of the base and twice on the strips.

Baking

Bake at 210C (400F) about 15 minutes. Immediately transfer to a cooling rack.

No. 18 Mini-Pizzas

Equipment

Baking sheet, rolling pin, plain round 5cm (2in) pastry cutter, knife, mixing bowl, pastry brush, cutting board, fork, teaspoon, pastry scraper, roller-docker.

Ingredients

Pizza dough, pizza sauce, salt, pepper, marjoram, mushrooms, tomatoes, cheese, black olives, egg glaze, olive oil.

Pizza Dough

1kg (2lb) flour, 15g (1/2oz) fresh yeast, 1/4L (1 cup) milk, 5 g (1 tsp) salt, 1 egg, 100g (3 1/2oz) butter melted with 8 cl (1/3 cup) olive oil.

Pizza Sauce

10cl (1/2 cup) olive oil, 1kg (2lb) onions, 1kg (2lb) peeled tomatoes, 6 cloves garlic, 100g (3 1/2oz) tomato paste, 1 bouquet garni (8 parsley stems, 3 thyme sprigs, 1/2 bay leaf, leek green), salt, pepper, sugar.

Procedure

Roll out the pizza dough to 3mm (1/8in) and prick it. Cut out the pizzas with the cutter. Remove the trimmings.

Turn the shapes over and lay them on a moistened baking sheet.

Brush them once with egg glaze.

Leave to rise slightly at room temperature.

Filling

Place a teaspoon (15g (1/2oz)) of pizza sauce on the base of each dough shape. Spread the sauce

evenly using a fork.

Lay a slice of tomato the same size as the dough shape on top of the sauce. Season with salt, pepper, and marjoram.

Place a 2cm (3/4in) square, 3mm (1/8in) thick piece of cheese on each pizza. Lay a strip of mushroom on top and add a drop or two of olive oil.

Baking

Bake in a very hot oven (250C (550F)) for 7-8 minutes, without drying out the pizzas.

Immediately after removing from the oven, put a piece of black olive on top. With the pastry brush, coat the olive with a little olive oil to keep it shiny.

Immediately transfer to a cooling rack.

No. 19 "Gougères"

Equipment

Saucepan, mixing bowl, spatula, pastry scraper, sieve, baking sheet, pastry bag and medium and small tips, pastry brush, whisk.

Ingredients

Cream puff pastry, egg glaze, grated swiss cheese, parmesan sauce.

Procedure

Make the cream puff pastry.

Using the medium tip, pipe out staggered rows of 2cm (3/4in) pastry puffs.

Brush the puffs with egg glaze and sprinkle the tops with grated swiss cheese. Remove the excess cheese by turning the baking sheet on its side.

Baking

Bake at 210C (400F) with the oven door slightly ajar for 15-20 minutes.

Immediately transfer to a cooling rack.

Parmesan Sauce

1/2L (2 cups) milk, 60g (2oz) butter, 2 eggs, 40g (1 1/2oz) cornstarch, 125g (4oz) grated swiss or parmesan cheese.

Filling

Pierce a hole in the side of the cream puffs.

Using the pastry bag fitted with the small tip, fill the puffs with parmesan sauce.

No. 20 "Croque Monsieurs"

Filling

With the palette knife, spread each slice of bread with parmesan sauce. Lay the slices of ham on top. Then cover them with more sauce. Generously sprinkle with grated swiss cheese and press lightly with the rectangle of wood to stick the swiss cheese.

Trim the sides with the knife then cut into 3.5cm (1 1/2in) x 4cm (1 3/4in) shapes.

Dip the bottom of each shape in the quiche batter to moisten the bread, then arrange on the buttered baking sheet.

Variation A

Equipment

Serrated knife, pastry brush, mixing bowl, rulers, palette knife, pastry scrapers, flat rectangle of wood, buttered baking sheet.

Ingredients

Square or rectangular loaf of white bread, parmesan sauce, grated swiss cheese, ham sliced 3mm (1/8in) thick, quiche batter, melted butter

Procedure

Cut 1.5cm (1/2in) slices from the loaf of bread using the serrated knife or a slicer.

Variation B

Equipment

Serrated knife, pastry brush, mixing bowl, ruler, palette knife, pastry scraper, flat rectangle of wood, buttered baking sheet.

Ingredients

Square or rectangular loaf of white bread, parmesan sauce, grated swiss cheese, ham sliced 3mm (1/8in) thick, melted butter.

Procedure

Cut 6mm (1/4in) slices from the loaf of white bread using the serrated knife or a slicer.

Filling

Using the small palette knife, spread each slice with the parmesan sauce.

Sprinkle with grated swiss cheese.

Lay the ham on half the slices of bread and cover with the other slices, cheese-side down.

Using the piece of wood, press lightly to seal.

Trim the edges of the bread. Cut the croque-monsieur into 3,5 cm × 4 cm (1 1/2in × 1 3/4in) shapes.

With the pastry brush, coat the tops of the shapes with melted butter.

Turn each piece over and arrange on the buttered baking sheet.

Coat the other side of the shapes with melted butter.

Baking

Bake at 210C (400F) about 4 minutes. Immediately transfer to a cooling rack. Trim the shapes.

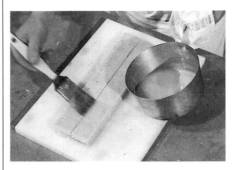

Baking

Bake at 210C (400F) about 5 minutes.

Immediately transfer to a cooling rack.

E - Mini Tartelettes

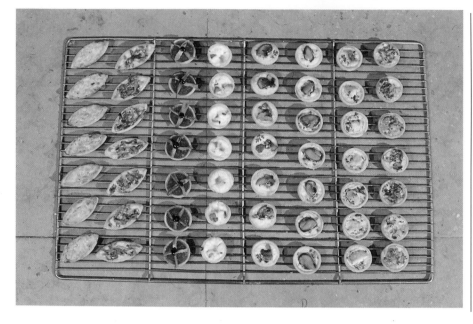

This family of hors d'œuvres provides a wide variety of flavors. Mini tartelette molds, round and barquette (boat shaped), are lined with basic pie pastry. The molds can be lined with pastry in advance and kept frozen until they are ready to be filled and baked. The filling is usually cheese, fish or vegetables that are baked with a light custard which makes these savory tartelettes very delicate and delicious.

These tartelettes bake at 210C (400F) just long enough to cook the pastry and set the custard without drying them out. Remove the pastries from the molds as soon as they come out of the oven so that the humidity from the custard does not make the crust soggy.

No. 21 Onion/Roquefort Tartelettes

Using a small spoon, fill the lined molds with custard/onion mixture to just below the rim. (Use 300g (10oz) onion compote for every 1/2L (2 cups) custard.)

Onion Compote: 75g (2 1/2oz) clarified butter, 1 kg (2lb) onions, 1 bouquet garni, salt, pepper.

Roquefort Custard

250g (8oz) creamed roquefort, 4dl (1 2/3 cups) heavy cream, 3dl (1 1/4 cups) milk, 7 eggs, salt, pepper, nutmeg.

Baking

Bake at 210C (400F) for about 15 minutes.

Remove from the molds and set on a cooling rack.

Equipment

Barquette molds, round baking sheets, rolling pin, brush, roller-docker, paring knife, mixing bowl, whisk, pastry scraper, oval pastry cutter.

Ingredients

Pie pastry, roquefort custard, onion compote.

Procedure

Make the pastry and line the molds. Chill at least one hour so that the pastry will not shrink when baked. Cook the onions until very soft, then cool. Mix the roquefort custard with the cooked onions.

No. 22 Salmon Tartelettes

Equipment

Tartelette molds, round baking sheets, rolling pin, brush, roller-docker, mixing bowl, whisk, pastry scraper, fork, knife, pastry cutter, funnel (specially designed funnels are available from professional equipment shops) or spoon.

Ingredients

Pie pastry, spinach, fresh salmon, salmon tartelette custard.

Procedure

Make the pastry and line the molds. Chill at least one hour so that the pastry will not shrink when baked.

Filling

Remove stems from the washed spinach and sauté in butter with a pinch of salt. Chop coarsely and cool. Using a fork, fill the bottom

Salmon Tartelette Custard

2dl (3/4 cup) milk, 1/4L (1 cup) heavy cream, 1 dl (1/2 cup) reduced "Americaine" sauce, 5 eggs, salt, pepper, small pinch of saffron.

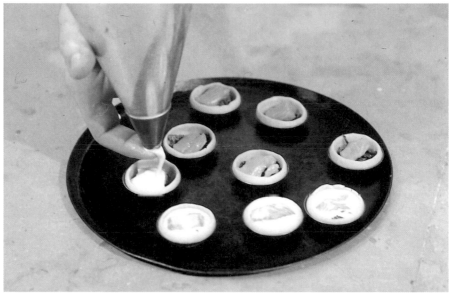

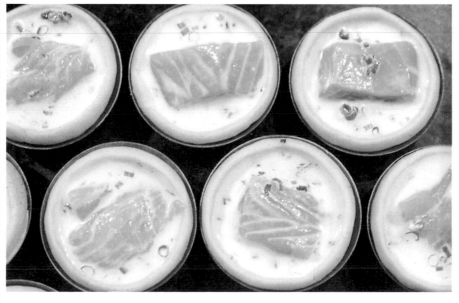

of each lined mold with a little spinach.

Place a small rectangle of fresh salmon on top of spinach. With a spoon or the funnel fill the tartelettes almost to the rim with the custard.

Baking

Bake at 210C (400F) about 15 minutes.

Immediately transfer to a cooling rack.

No. 23 Mussel Tartelettes

Equipment

Tartelette molds, round baking sheets, rolling pin, brush, roller-docker, mixing bowl, whisk, pastry scraper, paring knife, pastry cutter, funnel or spoon.

Ingredients

Pie pastry, mushroom duxelles, mussels "marinières", saffron quiche custard.

Mushroom Duxelles

30g (1oz) clarified butter, 45g (1 1/2oz) shallots, 200g (7oz) mushrooms, salt, pepper.

Saffron Quiche Custard

1/4L (1 cup) milk, 1/4L (1 cup) heavy cream, 5 eggs, salt, pepper, small pinch saffron.

Procedure

Make the pastry and line the molds. Chill at least one hour so that the pastry will not shrink when baked. Fill the bottom of each lined mold with a small spoonful of duxelles. Place a cooked mussel on top of the duxelles. Fill the mold almost to the rim with custard using the funnel or a spoon.

Baking

Bake at 210C (400F) about 15 minutes. Immediately transfer to a cooling rack.

No. 24 Mushroom Tartelettes

Equipment

Tartelette molds, round baking sheets, rolling pin, brush, roller-docker, mixing bowl, whisk, pastry scraper, pastry cutter, funnel or spoon.

Ingredients

Pie pastry, sautéed sliced mushrooms, quiche custard, sprigs of chervil.

Procedure

Make the pastry and line the molds. Chill at least one hour so the pastry will not shrink when baked.

Quiche Custard

1/2L (2 cups) heavy cream, 5 eggs, salt, pepper, nutmeg.

Filling

With a spoon place some sautéed sliced mushrooms in the bottom of each lined mold. Fill the molds just to the rim with custard using the funnel or a spoon. Garnish with chervil.

Baking

Bake at 210C (400F) about 15 minutes.

Immediately transfer to a cooling rack.

No. 25 Mini Quiches

Equipment

Tartelette molds, round baking sheets, rolling pin, brush, roller-docker, mixing bowl, whisk, pastry scraper, pastry cutter.

Ingredients

Pie pastry, diced ham, diced swiss cheese, diced bacon, quiche custard

Procedure

Make the pastry and line the molds. Chill at least one hour so that the pastry will not shrink when baked.

Blanch the diced bacon, then sauté the bacon and the ham in clarified butter.

Quiche Custard

1/2L (2 cups) heavy cream, 5 eggs, salt, pepper, nutmeg.

Filling

Place 1 cube of ham, 1 cube of bacon and 1 cube of cheese in each lined mold.

Fill the molds just to the rim with the quiche custard using the funnel or a spoon.

Baking

Bake at 210C (400F) about 15 minutes.

Immediately transfer to a cooling rack.

33

No. 26 "Pissaladières"

Equipment

Tartelette molds, round baking sheets, rolling pin, brush, roller-docker, mixing bowl, whisk, pastry scraper, small spoon, pastry brush, pastry cutter.

Ingredients

Pie pastry, pizza sauce, anchovy fillets, olives, olive oil.

Procedure

Make the pastry and line the molds. Chill at least one hour so that the pastry does not shrink when baked.

Pizza Sauce

1dl (1/2 cup) olive oil, 1kg (2lb) onions, 1kg (2lb) peeled tomatoes, 6 cloves garlic, 100g (3 1/2oz) tomato concentrate, 1 bouquet garni (8 parsley stems, 3 sprigs of thyme, 1/2 bay leaf, leek greens), salt, pepper, sugar.

Filling

With a small spoon, fill tartelette molds just to the rim with pizza sauce.

Baking

Bake at 210C (400 F) 15-20 minutes. Immediately transfer to a cooling rack.

Assembly

On each pizza, lay two thin strips of anchovy to form a cross.

Put a piece of olive in the center.

Brush the olive with olive oil to keep it shiny.

No. 27 Tartelettes of Julienned Vegetables

Equipment

Barquette molds, round baking sheets, rolling pin, brush, roller-docker, fork, mixing bowl, whisk, pastry scraper, funnel or spoon, pastry cutter.

Ingredients

Pie pastry, julienned vegetables with basil, quiche custard.

Procedure

Make the pastry and line the molds. Chill at least one hour so that the pastry does not shrink when baked.

Cut the vegetables in fine julienne,

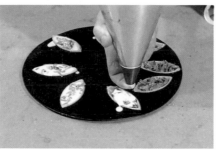

sauté until tender, set aside to cool.

Julienned Vegetables with Basil

250g (8oz) carrots, 150g (5oz) mushrooms, 200g (7oz) leeks (white part only), 15 leaves basil, 30g (1oz) clarified butter, salt, pepper.

Quiche Custard

1/2L (2 cups) heavy cream, 5 eggs, salt, pepper.

Filling

Using a small fork, put some julienned vegetable mixture in the bottom of each lined mold. Fill the molds just to the rim with the quiche custard using the funnel or a spoon.

Baking

Bake at 210C (400F) about 10 minutes. Immediately transfer to a cooling rack.

No. 28 Endive and Chive Tartelettes

Equipment

Tartelette molds, round baking sheets, rolling pin, brush, roller-docker, small spoon, mixing bowl, whisk, pastry scraper, spatula, knife, pastry cutter, funnel or spoon.

Ingredients

Pie pastry, belgian endive and chive mixture, quiche custard.

Procedure

Make the pastry and line the molds. Chill at least one hour so that the pastry does not shrink when baked. Slice the endive in small pieces and cook until soft, set aside to cool, then stir in garden chives.

Belgian Endive and Chive Mixture

30g (1oz) clarified butter, 250g (8oz) endives, salt, pepper, sugar, 10 sprigs chives.

Quiche Custard

1/2L (2 cups) heavy cream, 5 eggs, salt, pepper.

Filling

Using a small spoon place some endive/chive mixture in the bottom of each lined mold. Fill the molds just to the rim with the quiche custard using a funnel or a spoon.

Baking

Bake at 210C (400F) about 15 minutes.

Immediately transfer to a cooling rack.

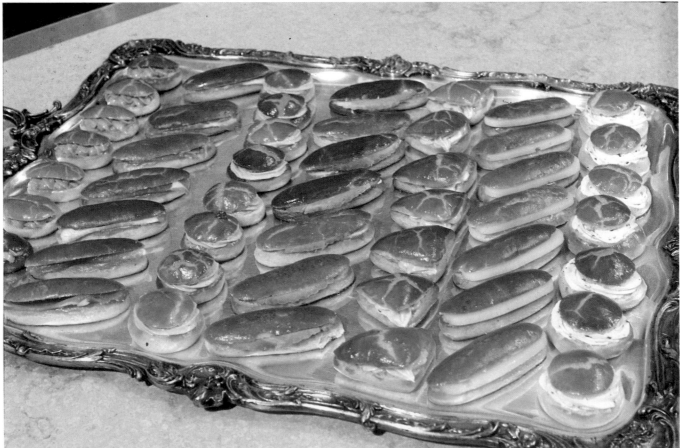

Chapter 2
Mini-Sandwiches and Filled Rolls

These sandwiches are popular with customers and caterers for the following reasons:

- they are easy and quick to prepare

- the food cost is relatively low

- their freshness adds a light touch to a buffet with heavier cooked dishes

- there are endless possibilities for shapes and fillings

Enjoyed by all, they are especially popular with younger guests.

The sandwiches outlined in this chapter can be transformed into " pains surprises " (surprise breads), which are described in detail in Chapter 6 on centerpieces.

General Advice for the Mini-Sandwiches

Baking and Shaping the Breads

These elegant little sandwiches can be made with a variety of breads to complement the taste of the filling.

The examples in this chapter are made with a classic white bread called "pain de mie", which literally means "bread of crumb" because of the fine close texture of the bread. This white bread is enriched with milk and butter which makes it moist and easy to slice.

In France, pain de mie is usually baked in 4-sided rectangular molds or closed cylinders, creating an even texture and neat shapes that are easily sliced into uniform squares, rectangles, triangles or circles. Alternatively, the bread can be baked in a regular loaf pan or high-sided pastry ring.

This delicious all-purpose white bread goes well with any filling.

Rye bread or whole wheat bread are also popular choices. These are sometimes augmented with nuts or herbs to enhance the filling. For example, a walnut bread goes well with roquefort, as shown in the chapter on canapés. Additional information on specialty breads is given in Chapter 6, which features centerpieces.

In all cases, the bread should be made 24 hours in advance, allowing it to cool completely before being sliced.

The thin slices needed for these delicate sandwiches are best achieved with a long sharp serrated knife or an electric slicer. The bread can also be made in sizeable batches and frozen, unsliced, for future use.

Once sliced, either fill sandwiches immediately or wrap the sliced loaves in plastic wrap and store in a cool place until ready to use. If you are not baking the breads yourself, select fresh, top quality breads.

A Variety of Fillings

A great variety of fillings can be used to make these sandwiches. The ingredients most often used are listed below, divided into four categories.

The fillings can be simple or sophisticated according to the taste and budget of the customer and the creativity of the caterer, ranging from an austere slice of good quality ham to roquefort butter with walnuts.

Even the most simple filling can be made special with a flavored butter or mayonnaise.

Preparation

After the breads for mini-sandwiches have been cut in thin even slices (about 6 mm (1/4in)), they need to be kept on damp hand towels or moistened parchment paper to keep them from drying out.

The procedure for assembling the sandwiches is essentially the same for all the fillings. In most cases, the slices are spread with a thin coating of softened butter or mayonnaise before the filling is added.

This coating holds the sandwiches together and keeps them moist and serves as well to protect the bread from absorbing juices from the filling. To personalize the sandwiches, this butter or mayonnaise can be accented with herbs or other flavorings. The exception is when the filling itself is a flavored butter or other creamy mixture like mousse of foie gras.

The mini-sandwiches can be assembled and shaped quickly by applying the filling to a whole band of bread at once. After laying the second layer of bread on top and pressing gently to seal, the filled bands can be stacked so that several sandwiches are shaped at the same time.

For all mini-sandwiches it is very important to use enough filling so that they are delicious and moist. However, too much filling spoils their appearance and makes them hard to handle.

General Categories of Sandwich Fillings

a) **Fish and shellfish:** smoked salmon, salmon butter, crab, tuna, potted shrimp

b) **Poultry, cold cuts, meats:** chicken, boiled or baked ham, smoked or dried ham, Bayonne ham, Parma ham, salami, dried sausage, mortadella, foie gras (mousse, purée), rillettes (potted meat), country pâté, liver pâté

c) **Crudités:** shredded lettuce and egg, mixed crudités: lettuce, tomato and egg; lettuce, tomato and cucumber; lettuce, carrot and celery

d) **Cheese:** herbed fresh cheese (or cottage cheese), roquefort butter with walnuts, comté, gruyère, beaufort, emmenthal or other swiss cheese

Presentation

These sandwiches can be arranged in neat rows on platters for buffets and receptions or sold individually in specialty food shops.

When sold individually, they are wrapped in plastic wrap or waxed paper to keep them fresh until they are purchased.

Once assembled, these sandwiches should be served within 12 hours. Keep them chilled on damp towels to keep them fresh until ready to serve.

Ham Sandwiches

Choose a good quality boiled or baked ham. Trim all the fat from the outside. Slice the ham thinly.

Stack several slices neatly on top of one another and trim all the slices at once to the width of the slice of bread.

The trimmings can be used to make a ham mousse, can be used in salads or in quiches.

Butter both slices of bread. Assemble the sandwiches. Remove the crusts and cut into the desired shapes.

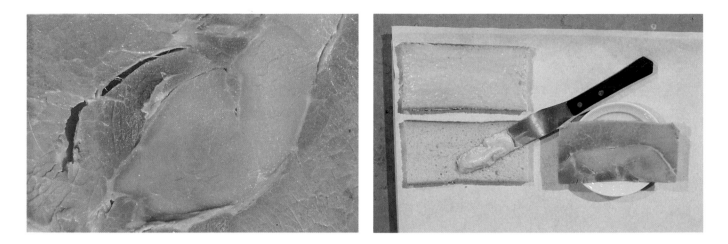

Swiss Cheese Sandwiches

Choose a flavorful swiss cheese with small or no holes so that the slices of cheese are more uniform and the sandwiches are even.

Good choices are Comté or Gruyère.

Remove the wax coating from the cheese. Slice it thinly and proceed as with ham sandwiches.

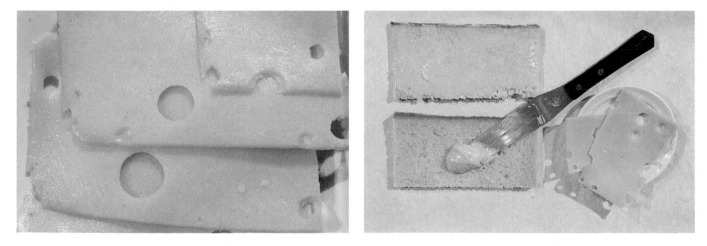

Sandwiches with Foie Gras Mousse

The foie gras for these sandwiches is usually purchased in a can. The label will indicate the percentage of foie gras in the preparation.

Since the foie gras is stirred until creamy, choose a " mousse ", " crème " or " purée ", which are less expensive than foie gras " en bloc ". " Pâté " of foie gras usually contains only a small amount of foie gras and will not be as delicious.

To make the sandwiches, stir the foie gras until creamy.

Lightly butter the slices of bread with a palette knife and spread a thin layer of the foie gras.

Alternatively, some extra butter can be beaten into the foie gras and this mixture can be applied directly on the bread.

Cover with the second slice of bread. Trim the crusts and cut into the desired shapes.

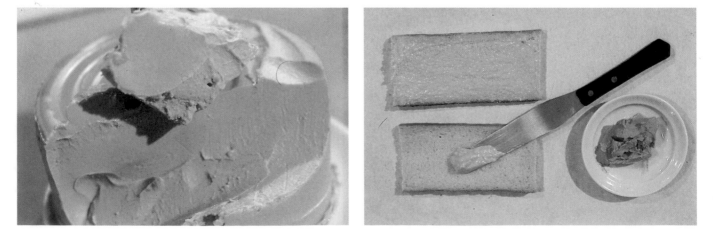

Lettuce and Tomato Sandwiches

The sliced bread is spread with mayonnaise, which goes well with the raw vegetables. The mayonnaise may be flavored with chopped fresh herbs: parsley, chervil, tarragon, chives.

Leaf lettuce is best to use, as it is the most tender and is easiest to eat. Sort and wash the lettuce leaves, then dry them carefully.

Remove any thick ribs, stack the leaves and slice into " chiffonade " (large julienne).

Select firm tomatoes so that the juice does not make the bread soggy.

Spread the slices of bread with the mayonnaise; cover with thin slices of tomato, then season with salt and pepper.

Arrange the shredded lettuce on top and cover with the second slice of bread. Remove the crusts and cut into desired shapes.

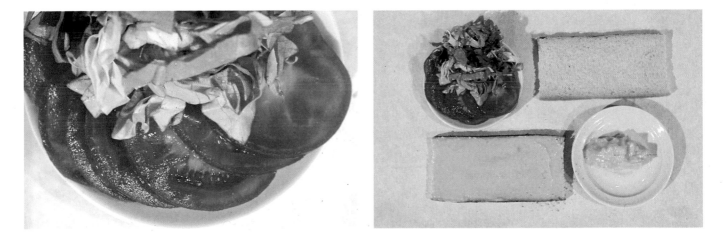

Salami Sandwiches

There are many different varieties of dried sausage available. Some are made in France, others in various European countries. Salami, made in Italy, is a thick long sausage that is ideal for use in sandwiches.

Peel away the skin, then slice the salami lengthwise, which will produce slices that correspond better to the shape of the bread and therefore will produce fewer trimmings and waste.

Spread the slices of bread with a thin layer of butter, lay the slice of salami on one slice of bread. Cover with the second slice. Remove the crusts and cut into the desired shapes.

Chicken Breast Sandwiches

Poach the whole chicken in chicken stock, which will keep the meat moist and prevent shrinkage. Leave to cool, remove the breast meat and cut it lengthwise into thin slices as shown.

Alternatively, poach only the

chicken breast (turkey breast may be used also); cool and slice as above.

Spread the slices of bread with mayonnaise, either plain or mixed with chopped fresh herbs or other seasonings, and arrange the slices of chicken on top. Cover with the

second slice of bread. Remove the crusts and cut into the desired shapes.

For efficiency and economy, a spread can be made using chopped meat from the whole chicken instead of only the sliced breast meat. Poach and cool the chicken, remove the fatty skin. Remove the meat from the chicken and cut into small pieces. Mix with mayonnaise and season with a pinch of curry powder or paprika. Spread generously on one slice of bread; cover with the second slice and press lightly to seal. Remove the crusts and cut into the desired shapes.

Mortadella Sandwiches

These sandwiches are made with mortadella, a flavorful sausage from Bologna, Italy which is about 15 cm (6in) in diameter, and is often studded with pistachios.

When sliced thinly, it is ideal for sandwiches.

Lay the sliced mortadella between the two slices of buttered bread. Remove the crusts and cut into the desired shapes.

Egg salad
(opposite page)

→

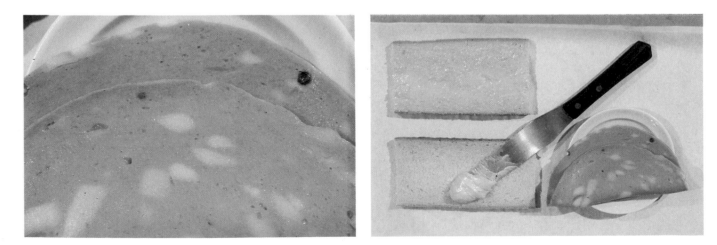

Egg Salad Sandwiches

The egg salad for these sandwiches is made from hard-boiled eggs that are peeled, then passed through a large-meshed sieve to create a fine texture.

To boil the eggs, place the raw eggs in a saucepan, cover with cold water and bring to a boil. Boil gently for 9 minutes, remove from the heat and leave under cold running water until the eggs are cool.

There are two ways to assemble these sandwiches: simply spread the two slices of bread with mayonnaise, top one slice with the sieved hard-boiled eggs (whites and yolks mixed together), garnish with some shredded lettuce, cover with the second slice and press lightly to seal. Remove the crusts and cut into the desired shapes.

For the second method, carefully mix the sieved whites and yolks with shredded lettuce and mayonnaise. Using a palette knife, spread the mixture on one slice of bread; lay the second piece on top. Remove the crusts and cut into the desired shapes.

With either method, the ingredients need to be seasoned, as they tend to be bland. Add a pinch of curry powder, paprika or cayenne to the mayonnaise.

Lettuce and Cucumber Sandwiches

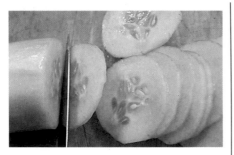

These sandwiches, which are part of the category of "crudités" sandwiches, are easy to make and use inexpensive ingredients. They are always popular because of their fresh taste and crisp texture.

Peel the cucumbers and slice them into thin rounds, about 3 mm (1/16 in).

It is not necessary to remove the seeds or degorge them (salting and leaving to drain in order to draw out excess juices) since the thin slices will be tender anyway. Furthermore, if the slices were degorged, they would become limp and make the sandwiches less crisp. As with all these sandwiches, use leaf lettuce.

Spread two slices of bread with well-seasoned mayonnaise and arrange the sliced cucumber on one slice. Cover with shredded lettuce and lay over the second slice of bread. Press lightly to seal; remove the crusts and cut into the desired shapes.

Crab Sandwiches

It is very important to choose good quality crab meat, which is often difficult to obtain. The price of good crab is generally high, so this must be reflected in the price of the sandwiches.

Canned crabmeat may be used, or use a whole crab poached in a court bouillon or fish stock. Leave the crab to cool, then carefully and thoroughly pick the meat from the shell. If using canned crab, drain it well, then flake it and remove any bits of shell or membrane.

Herb mayonnaise, especially made with chervil, is excellent with crab. Spread two slices of bread with the mayonnaise, then top one with the flaked crab meat.

Lay over the second slice of bread, press lightly to seal. Remove the crusts and cut into the desired shapes.

Alternatively, mix the crab and mayonnaise together and spread it directly on the bread.

Roquefort and Walnut Sandwiches

The choice of cheese is very important for these sandwiches. Choose a Roquefort that is very " blue " which will have lots of flavor. Pre-packaged Roquefort is not recommended because often it is quite bland.

Pass the cheese through a sieve or crush it with a fork, leaving it slightly lumpy.

Blend the cheese with half its weight in butter. Spread a thin layer of plain butter on two slices of bread to form a smooth surface, then spread one slice with the roquefort butter. Sprinkle with a generous layer of chopped walnuts, then cover with the second slice of bread. Remove the crusts and cut into the desired shapes.

Other blue cheeses may be used instead of Roquefort: Bleu-Stilton d'Auvergne, fourme d'Ambert, Gorgonzola or Danish Blue. The amount of butter added will depend on the texture and taste of the cheese used.

Chopped almonds or chopped grilled hazelnuts can be substituted for the walnuts. Raisins that have been blanched to soften them make a delicious complement to the flavor of the cheese.

When well-made and attractively arranged on platters in rows or rings, these sandwiches, as well as the others presented in this chapter, are always a welcome addition to a buffet menu.

General Advice for the Filled Rolls

The small rolls for these sandwiches are usually made with brioche or "pain au lait" (milk-enriched bread). These breads are made with milk and butter with the added richness of eggs.

The dough is refrigerated after the first rising. (The dough rises again a little in the refrigerator.)

Baking and Shaping the Bread

The butter in the chilled dough hardens, making it easy to roll out on a floured surface to a thickness of about 6 mm (1/4 in).

The sheet of dough is then cut into shapes with a pastry cutter. The most classic shape is oval, but they can also be cut in rounds or triangles. They can be cut by hand, but the rolls are usually more uniform if shaped with a pastry cutter.

For bite-size appetizer rolls, each piece of dough should weigh about 10 g (1/3oz).

Place the shaped dough in staggered rows on a baking sheet and leave to rise again before baking.

When risen, brush the top of these rolls with egg glaze which gives them a deep golden color.

Bake in a hot oven (210 C (400 F)) so they cook quickly without drying out.

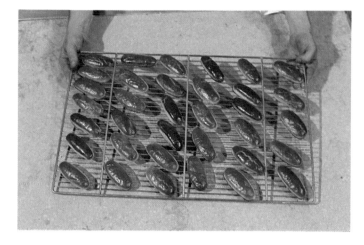

Larger shapes can be cut if the sandwiches will be served at a luncheon or sold in a specialty food store.

After they are baked, remove to a cooling rack to cool completely. If you are going to fill them right away, neatly slice the top 1/3 of the

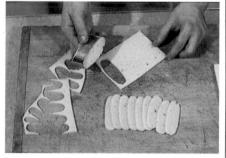

cooled rolls with a serrated knife. In some cases, the top is not cut through completely, leaving a " hinge " on one side that can be opened to fill the sandwiches.

53

They can be made in sizeable batches and frozen until needed. They are not sliced until just before they are filled. Arrange the rolls neatly in plastic boxes with tight-fitting lids.

A Variety of Fillings

As with the mini-sandwiches, the caterer can use a variety of fillings

to offer a wide assortment to the customer.

The most classic are simple fillings of sliced ham or cheese or more sophisticated mixtures of foie gras or creamy cheese with an addition of nuts or herbs.

For a neat and attractive appearance, the slices of ham and cheese can be cut with the same size cutter used to shape the rolls.

When making mixtures such as mousses that contain butter, an average proportion of butter is 1/2 the weight of the main ingredient.

Preparation

Once the tops are sliced, the interior is usually spread with a thin layer of softened butter or mayonnaise.

As with the mini-sandwiches, this coating is not necessary when the filling itself is creamy.

Be careful not to get butter or mayonnaise on the outside of the roll as this ruins the appearance.

As with the mini-sandwiches, be careful to use just enough filling to make a tasty sandwich.

Too much filling will make unattractive sandwiches that are too rich and difficult to handle.

For each roll weighing 10 g (1/3oz), count on about 10 g (1/3oz) of filling.

Pipe out the creamy fillings as uniformly as possible so they make an orderly arrangement on the platter.

In some cases the filling is then piped into the breads using a pastry bag and star tip.

Presentation

These small filled rolls are very attractive when placed in neat rows on a platter.

Remember to use different shapes filled with a variety of fillings for a lovely assortment.

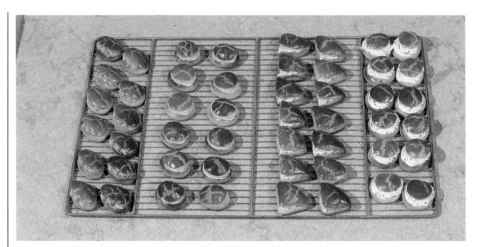

If the filled rolls are being sold in a specialty food shop, wrap them in plastic wrap or waxed paper. In all cases, chill until ready to serve.

Presentation on platters

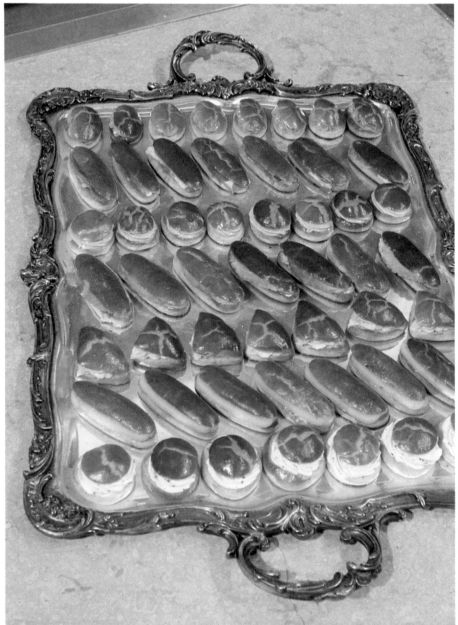

The 7 types of Filled Rolls

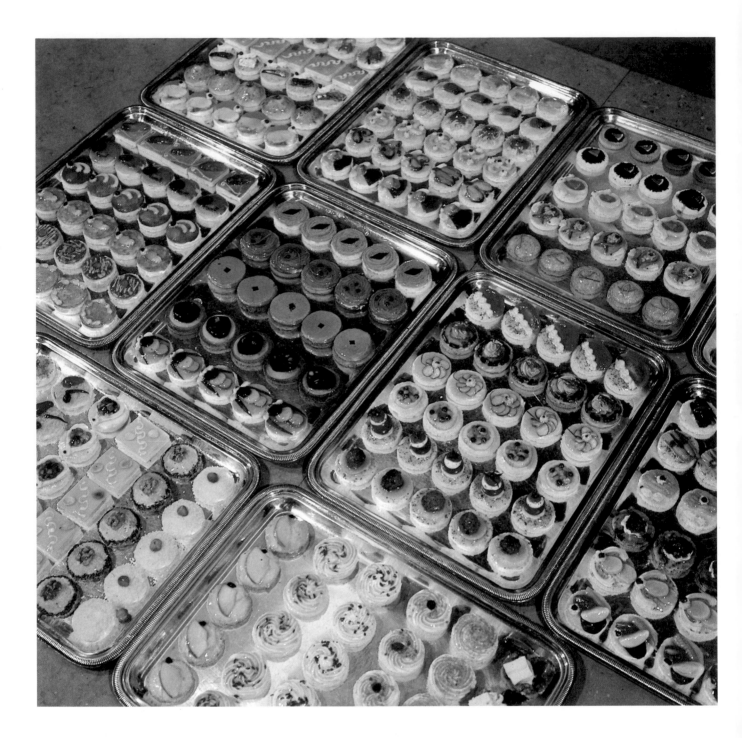

Chapter 3
Canapés

Canapés are a showcase for the talent and personality of the caterer. Indeed, you can say "Show me (and let me taste!) your canapés and I will tell you how good a caterer you are."

Canapés are not difficult to assemble. However, the professional caterer as well as those who appreciate fine food know that this specialty requires attention to the following details:

• The selection of top quality ingredients.

• The creation of innovative and pleasing taste combinations.

• The artistic and impeccable arrangement of the ingredients on each canapé for a well-balanced and stunning display.

• The organization of the many steps required to create these hors d'oeuvres within the busy schedule of the caterer.

Canapés are usually ordered for large receptions. The caterer's profit will often depend on how efficiently he can produce large numbers of these canapés.

Denis Ruffel shares with us 57 different canapés chosen from his vast collection of creations. This is a well-balanced selection using a variety of ingredients. Some of them are quick and simple to prepare, others require more technique and are more expensive to produce.

Here's an opportunity to add some new ideas to your repertoire of canapés.

Preparing the Bread for Canapés

The Bread Base

The base for classic canapés is usually made from "pain de mie", or basic enriched white bread, which is baked in a closed mold to create a close-textured bread. The milk and/or butter used to make this bread ensures a moist texture that is easy to slice. The thick crust protects the bread and keeps it fresher longer. You will see that for certain canapés, other close-textured breads are appropriate.

The Shape of the Bread

The bread can be baked in square, rectangular or round molds. It should be baked at least 24 hours in advance for easy slicing.

Slicing the Bread

The bread can be sliced by hand with a serrated bread knife, with an electric slicer or with a special electric bread slicer.

Keeping the Bread Fresh

Once the bread is sliced, it is important to wrap it in plastic wrap or moistened sheets of parchment paper to keep it from drying out.

The Thickness of the Slices

The thickness of the base may vary, but the bread is usually sliced 6 mm (1/4 in) thick.

The Shape of the Base

The slices of bread can be cut into a variety of shapes (hearts, diamonds, round) with different pastry cutters. Rectangular and square canapés are cut by hand with a serrated bread knife or with a tool with wires stretched across it, appropriately called a "guitar".

The crust, which keeps the bread fresh, should not be removed before the bases are cut out. The slices with the crust are sturdier and easier to work with.

Coating the Bread

Once the bread is cut into canapés, it is important to place them on sheets of moistened parchment paper to keep them from drying out. The next step for most canapés is to spread the top of the canapés with a thin layer of mayonnaise or creamed butter using a small palette knife. Depending on the canapé, this will be plain mayonnaise or butter or else a mixture flavored with herbs or other ingredients to enhance the flavor of the topping.

Some canapés are not coated with butter or mayonnaise when a mousse is used which is piped directly on the plain bread.

For square or rectangular canapés cut from rectangular slices of bread, it is possible to coat the whole slice, chill thoroughly to set before cutting into neat pieces with a serrated knife. When the coating will show as part of the final presentation, the serrated blade can be used to score a straight or swirled pattern into the butter or mayonnaise before cutting.

A few of the canapés use toasted bread as a base. In this case, melted butter is brushed on the bread,

Glazing the Canapés

Glazing the canapés

After the garnish is carefully placed on the coated bread base, it is possible, and indeed preferable, to brush on a thin coat of aspic to protect the canapés and to keep them moist.

It is necessary to thoroughly chill the canapés to set the garnish before brushing on the aspic.

Use a soft-bristled brush or goose feather to apply the aspic so that the delicate garnish is not damaged.

A Variety of Flavors

To improve the taste of the canapés, the aspic can be flavored to marry with the taste of the garnish (fish aspic with anise, chicken aspic with tarragon, aspic with madiera, sherry or port).

Storing the Canapés

Once the canapés have been brushed with the final aspic glaze, arrange them close together on moistened parchment paper and chill until ready to serve.

then the canapés are placed on a baking sheet and toasted in the oven until crisp and golden brown.

When the base is toasted it should not be placed on moistened parchment paper.

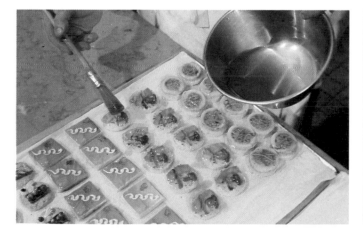

Selecting the Ingredients

The Choice of Ingredients

To make these canapés, the caterer works with a vast selection of ingredients which, when cleverly combined, provide a tempting array of products that are as beautiful to look at as they are delicious to eat.

The ingredients can be divided into categories, described here along with some useful advice.

Raw Vegetables

Radishes, cucumbers, tomatoes, for example. Purchase vegetables that are in season, perfectly ripe and unblemished. It is preferable to choose small vegetables, as large ones tend to be less firm and not as full flavored.

Cooked Vegetables

Fresh or canned vegetables can be used. For fresh ones, wash them thoroughly before cutting into the desired shapes. In most cases, they are cooked by plunging them into lightly salted boiling water, then refresh under cold running water to stop the cooking and fix their color.

The vegetables frequently found in cans or jars include small asparagus tips, artichokes, corn and hearts of palm.

Fruits

Apples, oranges, lemons, grapes, for example. Select only ripe unblemished fruits. The choice of fruit will depend on how their acidity and flavor combine with the other ingredients on the canapé.

Fish and Fish Products

Smoked Fish

(salmon, eel, trout...)
Make sure that the fish has been evenly and not too strongly smoked.

Marinated Fish

If you are going to marinate the fish yourself, allow enough time in advance. If you are purchasing the fish, confirm that the fish has been properly marinated and has a fresh smell and is moist.

Fresh Fish

Fresh fish should be purchased at the last moment and kept packed in crushed ice until ready to use.

Fish Eggs

Generally, caviar, salmon or lumpfish eggs are sold in cans or jars and sometimes need to be kept chilled. The high price of caviar means that it should be used sparingly.

Eggs

Quail eggs are used as well as hen's eggs. The eggs can be cut into slices, quartered or chopped.
Be sure that all eggs are perfectly fresh and are used quickly.

Preserved Meats

Choose fresh, top quality preserved meats.

Hams: Whole baked or boiled ham or Parma ham.
Sausages: Hard sausages flavored with garlic, andouilles, boudins.
Specialty: Liver pâté, "rillettes" (potted meats), foie gras or liver mousse.

Cheeses

Plain: Comté, Beaufort (or full flavored swiss cheese), goat cheese.

Mixed: Roquefort, Parmesan, Gorgonzola, cream cheese, fresh cheese with herbs.

A number of cheeses can be used to make canapés. Choose properly aged cheese that is not too ripe or too strong, as the odor will penetrate the other canapés around it.

The 57 Canapés

Top Platter

In order from left to right and top to bottom:

1. Sole mousse with herbs - 2. Fresh salmon - 3. Smoked salmon
4. Sardine - 5. Tuna - 6. Monkfish - 7. Eel - 8. Pickled herring
9. Crab - 10. Shrimp - 11. Mussels - 12. Bay scallops - 13. Caviar -
14. Lumpfish eggs - 15. Salmon eggs - 16. Anchovy - 17. Tarama -
18. Smoked trout - 19. Salmon mousse

Bottom Platter

In order from left to right and top to bottom:

20. Hard-boiled egg - 21. Quail egg - 22. Egg salad - 23. Boiled
ham - 24. Parma ham - 25. Tongue - 26. Garlic sausage - 27. Dry
sausage - 28. Andouille - 29. Liver mousse - 30. Duck mousse -
31. Foie gras - 32. Blood sausage and apple - 33. Mixed sausages

Of Denis Ruffel

Top Platter

In order from left to right and top to bottom:

34. Tomato - **35.** Sautéed zucchini - **36.** Radish - **37.** Cucumber - **38.**
Cherry tomato - **39.** Raw turnip - **40.** Green beans
41. Asparagus tips - **42.** Artichoke bottoms - **43.** Broccoli - **44.** Hearts
of palm - **45.** Baby corn - **46.** Mushrooms - **47.** Sweet pepper
48. Macédoine

Bottom Platter

In order from left to right and top to bottom:

49. Comté - **50.** Roquefort - **51.** Parmesan - **52.** Gorgonzola
53. Munster cream - **54.** "Fromage frais" with chives - **55.** "Fromage
frais" with walnuts and raisins - **56.** "Fromage frais" with paprika -
57. Goat cheese

65

The Repertoire of Canapés by Category

Name of Canapé	Main Ingredients	Preparation Time	Food Cost	Level of Difficulty
1. Sole mousse with herbs	Fish/fresh herbs	–––––	★★	★★
2. Fresh salmon	Fresh fish	––––	★	★
3. Smoked salmon	Smoked fish	–––	★★	★
4. Sardine	Preserved fish	–––	–	–
5. Tuna	Preserved fish	–––	–	–
6. Monkfish	Fish and citrus	––––––	★★	★★
7. Smoked eel	Smoked fish	–––––	★★	★
8. Pickled herring	Preserved fish	–––––	★	★
9. Crab	Preserved fish and vegetables	–––––	★★	★
10. Shrimp	Shellfish	––––	★	–
11. Mussels	Shellfish	––––	★	★
12. Bay scallops	Shellfish	––––	★	★
13. Caviar	Fish eggs	––	★★	–
14. Lumpfish eggs	Fish eggs	––	–	–
15. Salmon eggs	Fish eggs	––	★★	–
16. Anchovy	Preserved fish	––	★	–
17. Tarama	Fish eggs	––	★	–
18. Smoked trout	Smoked fish	–––––	★	★
19. Salmon mousse	Smoked fish	–––––	★	★
20. Hard-boiled eggs	Eggs	––	––	––
21. Quail eggs	Eggs	––	–	–
22. Egg salad	Eggs	–––	––	–
23. Boiled ham	Preserved meats	–	–	––
24. Parma ham	Preserved meats	––––	★★	★
25. Tongue	Preserved meats	––	★★	–
26. Garlic sausage	Preserved meats	–	––	––
27. Dry sausage	Preserved meats	–	––	––
28. Andouille	Preserved meats	–	★	––
29. Liver mousse	Liver mousse	––	★	–
30. Duck mousse	Duck	–––––	★	★
31. Foie gras	Foie gras	–––	★★	★
32. Blood sausage with apple	Blood sausage	––––––	★	★
33. Mixed sausages	Mixed sausages	––––––	★★	★
34. Tomato	Raw vegetables	–	––	––
35. Sautéed zucchini	Raw vegetables	––––––	★	★
36. Radish	Raw vegetables	–––––	––	
37. Cucumber	Raw vegetables	–––	–	–
38. Cherry tomato	Raw vegetables	––––––	★★	★
39. Turnip	Raw vegetables	––––––	★	★
40. Green beans	Raw vegetables	–––	–	––
41. Asparagus tips	Canned vegetables	––	★	–
42. Artichoke bottoms	Canned vegetables	–	★	––
43. Broccoli	Raw vegetables	–––	★	–
44. Hearts of palm	Canned vegetables	–	–	––
45. Baby corn	Raw vegetables	––––––	★★	★★
46. Mushrooms	Canned vegetables	––	–	––
47. Sweet pepper	Canned vegetables	––––––	★	★
48. Macédoine	Raw vegetables	–––––	–	–
49. Comté	Cheese	––	–	–
50. Roquefort	Cheese	––	★	–
51. Parmesan	Cheese	––––	★	–
52. Gorgonzola	Cheese	––	★	–
53. Munster cream	Cheese	–––	★	–
54. "Fromage frais" w/chives	Cheese	––	–	–
55. "Fromage frais" w/walnuts and raisins	Cheese	––	★	–
56. "Fromage frais" w/paprika	Cheese	––	–	–
57. Goat cheese	Cheese	––––––	★★	★

Detailed Description of Each Canapé

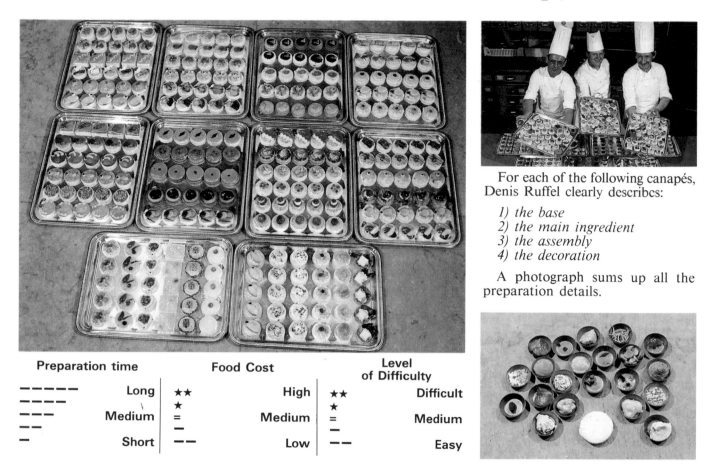

For each of the following canapés, Denis Ruffel clearly describes:

1) the base
2) the main ingredient
3) the assembly
4) the decoration

A photograph sums up all the preparation details.

Preparation time		Food Cost		Level of Difficulty	
－－－－－	Long	★★	High	★★	Difficult
－－－－		★		★	
－－－	Medium	=	Medium	=	Medium
－－		－		－	
－	Short	－－	Low	－－	Easy

No. 1 Canapés of Sole Mousse with Herbs

Base

Round canapé of lightly buttered white bread, spread with a thin coat of saffron mayonnaise

Main Ingredients

"Paupiette" of sole with herbs that has been prepared one day in advance

Fish mousse (for 6 filets of sole: 100 g (3 1/2 oz) pike, perch or other flavorful white fish, 100 g (3 1/2 oz) heavy cream, 1 egg, 2 teaspoons chopped herbs (chervil, tarragon, chives), salt, cayenne pepper)

Assembly

Spread the mousse on the filets of sole. Roll into cylinders, wrap in plastic film and tie the two ends.

Poach in fish stock. Chill until ready to use.

Cut the "paupiettes" into slices 3 mm (1/8 in) thick and place them on the prepared canapés.

Decoration

Brush with aspic. Overlap a few thin strips of blanched lemon and lime zest on top. Brush with a second coat of aspic.

No. 2 Fresh Salmon Canapés

Base

Round canapé of lightly buttered white bread, spread with a thin coat of mayonnaise flavored with chopped tarragon

Main Ingredients

Small rectangle of fresh salmon poached in fish stock
Small chanterelle or other wild mushroom sautéed in butter

Assembly

Place the piece of poached salmon and the small mushroom on the prepared base.

Decoration

Brush once with aspic. Dip a leaf of fresh tarragon in aspic and lay it across the salmon.

Brush on another coat of aspic.

No. 3 Smoked Salmon Canapés

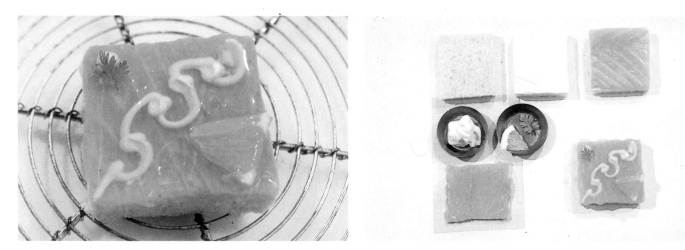

Base

Rectangular slice of lightly buttered white bread cut lengthwise from whole loaf

Main Ingredient

Thin slices (about 1.5 mm (1/16 in)) of smoked salmon trimmed to fit the slice of bread (Chill the salmon thoroughly before slicing)

Assembly

Place the salmon on the slice of buttered bread. Trim the crusts. Cut into squares or rectangles.

Decoration

Using a paper cone, pipe a delicate design with creamed salted butter across the salmon, as shown.
Brush with a coat of aspic.
Place a small triangle of lemon with all rind removed on one corner and a leaf of chervil in the opposite corner. Brush again with a second coat of aspic.

No. 4 Sardine Canapés

Base

Round canapé of white bread

Main Ingredient

Sardine butter (made from combining equal quantities of sardines and creamed butter, with adjusted seasonings)

Filet of sardine

Assembly

Using a small palette knife, spread the canapé with a 3 mm (1/8 in) slightly rounded layer of sardine butter.

Lay a sardine filet on top, slightly off center.

Decoration

Using a pastry bag fitted with a

small star tip, pipe a rosette of creamed salted butter, as shown. Place a caper on the butter.

No. 5 Tuna Canapés

Base

Round canapé of lightly buttered white bread.

Main Ingredients

Tuna mayonnaise (made from 1 part flaked tuna and 3 parts mayonnaise, seasoned with chopped parsley and curry powder)

Assembly

Using a small palette knife, spread a slightly rounded layer of tuna mayonnaise on the base.

Decoration

Lay a tiny slice of pickled onion in the center of the canapé and top with a sprig of parsley.

No. 6 Canapés of Monkfish Medallions

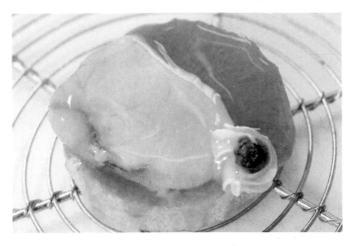

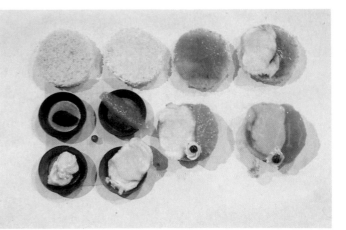

Base

Round canapé of lightly buttered white bread, spread with a thin layer of tomato mayonnaise

Main Ingredients

Monkfish poached "en ballotine" (Wrap a monkfish tail in plastic film and tie the ends tightly. Poach it in fish stock and leave to cool.)

Orange segments trimmed of all pith and peel

Assembly

Lay a 3 mm (1/8 in) slice of poached monkfish on one side of the prepared canapé. Lay the trimmed orange segment on the other side.

Decoration

Pipe a small rosette of creamed salted butter, as shown, and top with a green peppercorn. Brush on a coat of fish aspic.

No. 7 Smoked Eel Canapés

Base

Round canapé of lightly buttered white bread, spread with a thin layer of smoked eel butter

Main Ingredients

Smoked eel butter (made by mixing 1 part smoked eel and 4 parts butter, passing it through a fine sieve and adjusting the seasoning)

Small rectangle of skinned and boned smoked eel filet

Assembly

Lay the eel on the prepared base.

Decoration

Using a pastry bag fitted with a small star tip, pipe a decorative border of creamed salted butter, as shown. Lay a very thin slice of radish on top.

No. 8 Pickled Herring Canapés

Base

Round canapé of lightly buttered white bread, spread with a thin layer of mayonnaise

Main Ingredients

Pickled herring
Slice of carrot, cut with the waffle blade on the mandoline and

cooked in boiling salted water

Assembly

Lay a diamond-shaped piece of pickled herring on the prepared canapé and place the carrot slice on top.

Decoration

Place a sprig of chervil on the carrot and brush the canapé with a coat of aspic.

No. 9 Crab Canapés

Base

Round canapés of lightly buttered white bread, spread with a thin layer of mayonnaise

Main Ingredients

Avocado mousse (250 g (8 oz) avocado, lemon juice, 2 leaves softened gelatin, 1 dl (1/2 cup) whipped heavy cream, salt, cayenne pepper)
Flaked crab meat

Assembly

Using a pastry bag fitted with a medium plain tip, pipe a mound of avocado mousse in the center of the prepared canapé. Sprinkle the flaked crab around the edges.

Decoration

Put a salmon egg on top of the avocado mousse. Brush with a coat of aspic.

No. 10 Shrimp Canapés

Base

Round canapé of white bread spread with a thin layer of aurora butter

Main Ingredients

Aurora butter (100 g (3 1/2 oz) butter, 15 g (1/2 oz) tomato paste, a few drops cognac or vodka, salt, pepper, paprika)

Shelled shrimp

Assembly

Place three shrimps on the prepared canapé.

Decoration

Using a pastry bag fitted with a star tip, pipe rosettes of creamed salted butter, as shown.

Place a small piece of black olive in the middle of the central rosette, and using a paper cone, pipe a dot of tomato paste in the center of the three other rosettes.

Brush with a coat of aspic.

No. 11 Mussel Canapés

Base

Round canapés of lightly buttered white bread, spread with a thin layer of curry flavored mayonnaise

Main Ingredients

Mussels "marinières", fresh or from a jar. Cook chopped shallots and onions in butter until soft but not brown, add the mussels, add some dry white wine, a bouquet garni and some pepper. Cover the pot and cook until the mussels open. Cool and remove the mussels from the shells.

Assembly

Arrange two mussels in a fan shape on the prepared canapé.

Decoration

Using a pastry bag fitted with a small star tip, pipe a design of creamed salted butter, as shown.

Lay a small diamond of cooked red pepper in the center. Sprinkle a tiny pinch of snipped chives on the other side of the mussels.

Brush on a coat of aspic.

No. 12 Bay Scallop Canapés

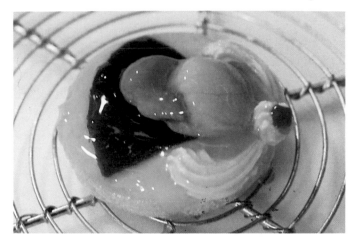

Base

Round canapés of lightly buttered white bread, spread with a thin coat of mayonnaise

Main Ingredients

Bay scallops poached in fish stock
Blanched leek (green portion)

Assembly

Placc a triangle of leek on the prepared canapé and top it with a poached scallop.

Decoration

Using a pastry bag fitted with a small star tip, pipe a decorative border using creamed salted butter, as shown. Using a paper cone, pipe a dot of tomato paste in the center of the butter design.

Brush on a coat of aspic.

No. 13 Caviar Canapés

Base

Round canapé of white bread, brushed with melted butter and toasted

Main Ingredient

Caviar

Assembly

Place a ring template as shown over the canapé to measure out the right amount and to center the garnish. Spread the inside of the ring with caviar.

Decoration

Top with a small triangle of lemon that has been completely trimmed of peel and pith.

No. 14 Canapés with Lumpfish Eggs

Base

Round canapé of lightly buttered white bread that has been thoroughly chilled so the round template doesn't stick to the butter

Main Ingredient

Lumpfish eggs

Assembly

Place a ring template on the canapé and gently spread the inside of the circle with lumpfish eggs.

Decoration

Top with a small triangle of lemon that has been completely trimmed of pith and peel.

No. 15 Canapés with Salmon Eggs

Base

Round canapé of lightly buttered white bread, spread with a thin layer of mayonnaise

Main Ingredient

Salmon eggs

Assembly

Using a pastry bag fitted with a small star tip, pipe a medallion of creamed salted butter with a rosette at one end, as shown.

Fill the center of the medallion with salmon eggs.

Decoration

Using a paper cone, pipe a dot of tomato paste in the center of the butter rosette and top the salmon eggs with a small triangle of lemon that has been completely trimmed of pith and peel.

No. 16 Anchovy Canapés

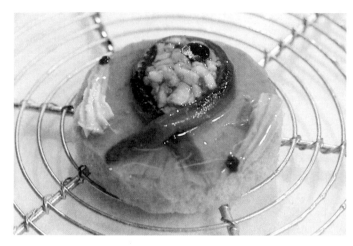

Base

Round canapé of white bread, spread with 1.5 mm (1/16 in) layer of anchovy butter

Main Ingredients

Anchovy butter (made by combining 1 part anchovy to 4 parts butter)
Anchovy filets
Chopped hard-boiled egg

Assembly

Arrange an anchovy filet in the shape of a fish on the prepared canapé.

Fill the inside of the fish with chopped hard-boiled egg.

Decoration

Using a pastry bag fitted with a small star tip, pipe creamed salted butter, as shown. Using a paper cone, pipe a dot of tomato paste on each shape. Place a small piece of red pepper on the fish as the eye.
Brush on a coat of aspic.

No. 17 Tarama Canapés

Base

Round canapé of white bread, brushed with melted butter and toasted

Main Ingredients

Tarama (made with 200 g (7 oz) cod roe, 1 cl (2 tsp) lemon juice,

3 cl (2 tbsp) oil, 6 cl (1/4 cup) heavy cream, salt, pepper)

Assembly

Using a small palette knife, spread a slightly rounded layer of tarama on the canapé. Flatten the top of the round.

Decoration

Top with a thin strip of blanched lime zest.

No. 18 Smoked Trout Canapés

Base

Round canapés of white bread

Main Ingredients

Smoked trout butter (made by combining 1 part smoked trout filet with 4 parts butter and passing through a fine sieve)

Smoked trout filet, skin and bones removed

Raw leek (white portion), sliced very thin

Assembly

Lay a diamond-shaped piece of smoked trout on the prepared canapé. On either side place a half slice of leek.

Decoration

Add a pinch of chopped hard-boiled egg white to one end and yolk to the other end.

Brush on a coat of aspic.

No. 19 Smoked Salmon Mousse Canapés

Base

Round canapé of white bread

Main Ingredient

Smoked salmon mousse (equal amounts smoked salmon and un-salted butter)

Assembly

Using a pastry bag fitted with a large star tip, pipe a rosette of smoked salmon mousse onto the canapé.

Decoration

Decorate with salmon eggs and a sprig of dill.

Brush on a coat of aspic.

No. 20 Hard-boiled Egg Canapés

Base

Round canapé of lightly buttered white bread, spread with a thin layer of mayonnaise

Main Ingredients

Hard-boiled egg
Truffle

Assembly

Cut the egg into slices using an egg slicer (1 egg yields approximately 5 slices). Lay a slice on the prepared canapé.

Decoration

Using a pastry bag fitted with a small star tip, pipe a small rosette of mayonnaise in the center of the egg slice. Top the rosette with a piece of truffle cut using a small round cutter.

Brush on a coat of aspic.

No. 21 Canapés with Quail's Eggs

Base

Round canapé of lightly buttered bread, spread with a thin layer of mayonnaise

Main Ingredient

Hard-boiled quail's eggs (fresh or from a jar)

Assembly

Cut the quail's eggs in half lengthwise. Place one half cut side up on the prepared canapé.

Decoration

Using a pastry bag fitted with a small star tip, pipe a design of mayonnaise around the egg, as shown.

Add a sprig of chervil on either side of the mayonnaise design and a dot of lumpfish eggs in the center of the mayonnaise.

Brush on a coat of aspic.

No. 22 Canapés with Egg Salad

Base and Main Ingredients

Round canapé of very lightly buttered white bread, spread with a thin layer of mayonnaise

Hard-boiled egg whites and yolks passed separately through a sieve

Parsley mayonnaise

Assembly

Using a pastry bag fitted with a star tip, pipe a ring of parsley mayonnaise in the center of the prepared canapé. Surround the mayonnaise with the egg white and carefully fill the center of the ring with the yolk.

Decoration

Place a caper in the center of the canapé.

Brush on a coat of aspic.

No. 23 Boiled Ham Canapés

Base

Buttered slice of white bread cut from the length of the loaf

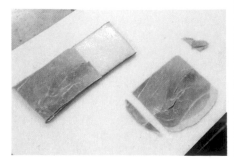

Main Ingredient

Boiled ham

Assembly

Cut the ham into 1.5 mm (1/16 in) slices trimmed to fit the bread. Trim off crusts.

Cut the slice into 5 cm × 4 cm (2 in × 1 3/4 in) rectangles.

Decoration

Slice a cornichon into a fan shape and lay it on the ham. Using a paper cone, pipe a design in creamed salted butter, as shown.

Brush on a coat of aspic.

No. 24 Parma Ham Canapés

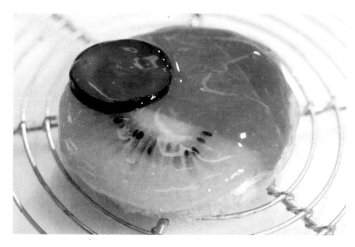

Base

Round canapé of buttered white bread

Main Ingredients

Parma ham
Kiwi

Assembly

Cut a thin slice of Parma ham to fit the canapé. Reserve the trimmings for another use. Cut it in two and overlap the two halves on the prepared canapé.

Cover the other side of the canapé with half of a thin slice of kiwi.

Decoration

Place a thin slice of black grape on top.

Brush on a coat of aspic.

No. 25 Tongue Canapés

Base

Round canapé of buttered white bread

Main Ingredient

Tongue

Assembly

Slice the tongue about 1.5 mm (1/16 in) thick and cut out shapes the size of the canapé. Reserve the trimmings for another use. Lay the rounds of tongue on the prepared canapé.

Decoration

Using a pastry bag fitted with a small star tip, pipe a design with creamed salted butter, as shown. Place a caper at the end of one crescent. On the other side of the canapé, lay a thin slice of pickled onion. Brush on a coat of aspic.

No. 26 Garlic Sausage Canapés

Base

Round canapés of buttered white bread

Main Ingredient

Garlic sausages

Assembly

Using a plain pastry cutter, stamp out a thin slice of sausage to the same size as the canapé and lay it on the prepared base.

Decoration

Using a pastry bag fitted with a small star tip, pipe a design in creamed salted butter, as shown.

Top with a small piece of black olive and a thin slice of pickled onion.

Brush on a coat of aspic.

No. 27 Dry Sausage Canapés

Base

Round canapé of buttered white bread.

Main Ingredient

Dry sausage

Assembly

Using a plain pastry cutter, stamp out a thin slice of sausage to the same size as the canapé and lay it on the prepared base.

Decoration

Using a paper cone, pipe a design in creamed butter, as shown, and top with a slice of cornichon.

Brush on a coat of aspic.

No. 28 Andouille Canapés

Base

Round canapés of buttered white bread

Main Ingredient

Andouille

Assembly

Cut out a thin slice of andouille to the same size as the canapé and lay it on the prepared base.

Decoration

Using a pastry bag fitted with a small star tip, pipe a design of creamed salted butter, as shown.

Top the center of the design with a slice of cornichon.

Brush on a coat of aspic.

No. 29 Liver Mousse Canapés

Base

Round canapé of very lightly buttered bread.

Main Ingredient

Liver mousse (to which butter may be added to achieve the desired consistency).

Assembly

Using a pastry bag fitted with a small star tip, pipe the mousse on the canapé in a spiral pattern.

Decoration

Top with a diamond-shaped slice of truffle.

Brush on a coat of aspic.

No. 30 Duck Mousse Canapés

cream, 1 cl (2 tsp) port, 45 g (1 1/2 oz) butter, salt, pepper)

Base

Round canapé of white bread, brushed with melted butter and toasted, then spread with a thin layer of salted butter

Main Ingredient

Duck mousse (made with 250 g (8 oz) cooked duck breast, 2 cl (4 tsp) duck glaze, 3 cl (2 tbsp) heavy

Assembly

Using a pastry bag fitted with a small star tip, pipe the mousse on the canapé in a spiral pattern.

Decoration

Top with 3 fine strips of blanched orange zest and 3 green peppercorns.

Brush on a coat of aspic.

No. 31 Foie Gras Canapés

Base

Round canapé of white bread, brushed with melted butter and toasted

Main Ingredient

Truffled foie gras

Assembly

Lay a slice of foie gras no thicker than 1 cm (3/8 in) and the same diameter as the canapé on the prepared base.

Decoration

Brush on a coat of aspic, covering the sides of the slice of foie gras, but not the sides of the toast.

No. 32 Canapés with Blood Sausage and Apples

Base

Round canapé of white bread, brushed with melted butter and toasted

Main Ingredients

Blood sausage
Apples
Unsweetened apple compote

Assembly

Using a plain pastry cutter, stamp out a slice of apple about 1.5 mm (1/16 in) thick. Stamp out the center of the slice using a small round cutter. Pan-fry the slices in clarified butter. Place the slice of apple on the canapé and fill the center with some apple compote. Put a 6mm (1/4 in) slice of blood sausage in the center of the canapé.

Decoration

Brush on a coat of aspic.

No. 33 Canapés with Mixed Sausages

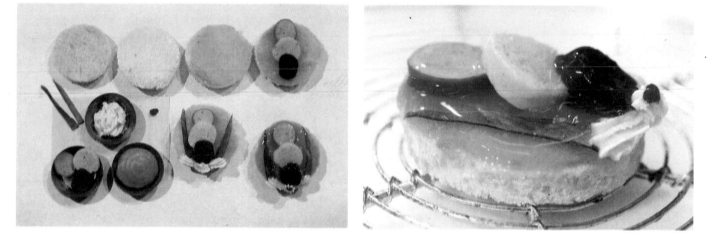

Base

Round canapé of very lightly buttered white bread, spread with a thin layer of unsweetened apple compote.

Main Ingredients

Cocktail frank
Mini veal sausage
Mini blood sausage

Assembly

Arrange a 6 mm (1/4 in) slice of each of the three sausages so they overlap slightly on the canapé.

Decoration

Lay a half leaf of tarragon along each side of the slices.

Using a pastry bag fitted with a small star tip, pipe a design with creamed salted butter as shown, and with a paper cone, pipe a dot of tomato paste on the butter design.

Brush on a coat of aspic.

No. 34 Tomato Wedge Canapés

Assembly

Place the tomato wedge on the prepared canapé.

Decoration

Using a pastry bag fitted with a small star tip, pipe a design with creamed salted butter, as shown, and using a paper cone, pipe a dot of tomato paste at one end of the butter.

Base and Main Ingredients
Round canapé of very lightly buttered white bread, spread with a

thin coat of herb mayonnaise

Tomato wedges cut from firm red tomatoes

No. 35 Sautéed Zucchini Canapés

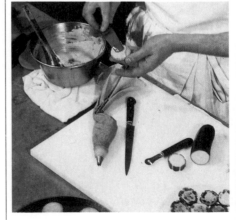

Base and Main Ingredients

Round canapé of white bread, brushed with melted butter and toasted

Zucchini, fluted slices cut 1 cm (3/8 in) thick
Salmon mousse (p. 76)

Assembly

Sauté the zucchini in olive oil. Spread the canapé with a thin layer of salmon mousse and cover with a slice of zucchini. Top the zucchini with a rosette of salmon mousse using a pastry bag fitted with a medium star tip.

Decoration

Place a sprig of dill on top. Brush on a coat of aspic.

No. 36 Radish Canapés

Base
Round canapé of buttered white bread

Main Ingredient

Radish

Assembly

Arrange very fine slices of radish in a flower pattern on the prepared canapé.

Using a pastry bag fitted with a small star tip, pipe a rosette of creamed salted butter in the center of the flower.

Top the rosette with a dot of tomato paste.

Decoration

Make a stem for the flower with a sprig of chive.

Brush on a coat of aspic.

No. 37 Canapés with Cucumber, Corn and Green Peppercorns

Base
Round canapé of lightly buttered white bread, spread with a thin coat of mayonnaise

Main Ingredients
Cucumber
Corn kernels
Green peppercorns in brine

Assembly

Slice the peeled cucumber into 6 mm (1/4 in) slices. With a small fluted pastry cutter, cut out the center of the sliced cucumber to remove the seeds.
Put the cucumber slice on the prepared canapé. Fill the middle with corn kernels and green peppercorns.

Decoration

Top with a chervil sprig.
Brush on a coat of aspic.

No. 38 Cherry Tomato Canapés

Base

Round canapé of very lightly buttered white bread, spread with a thin layer of herb mayonnaise. Using a pastry bag fitted with a small star tip, pipe a small circle of creamed salted butter to hold the cherry tomato in place.

Main Ingredients

Cherry tomatoes
"Fromage frais" (or cottage cheese passed through a fine sieve) with herbs

Assembly

Cut the tops of the tomatoes and with a small melon baller, remove the seeds. Set the tomato on the circle of butter. With a pastry bag fitted with a small plain tip, fill the tomatoes with the "fromage frais".

Decoration

Replace the tops of the tomatoes.

No. 39 Turnip Canapés

Base and Main Ingredients

Round canapé of very lightly buttered white bread, spread with a thin layer of herb mayonnaise
Turnips
Meat stuffing (veal, pork, herbs, seasonings)

Assembly

Slice the turnip in 6 mm (1/4 in) slices and cook in a little water with butter and sugar until glazed. Place a slice of the turnip on the prepared canapé.

Roll the meat stuffing into small balls, pan-fry them in clarified butter, and set one on top of each slice of turnip.

Decoration

Brush on a coat of aspic.

No. 40 Green Bean Canapés

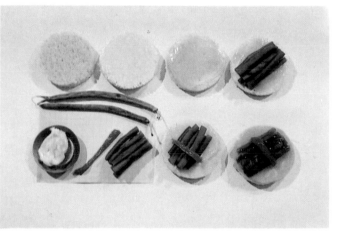

Base

Round canapé of very lightly buttered white bread, spread with a thin coating of mayonnaise

Main Ingredients

Extra thin green beans
Cooked red pepper

Assembly

Place a small bundle of cooked green beans cut to the same length on the prepared canapé.

Decoration

Lay a small strip of red pepper on the beans to form the tie.

Brush on a coat of aspic.

No. 41 Asparagus Tip Canapés

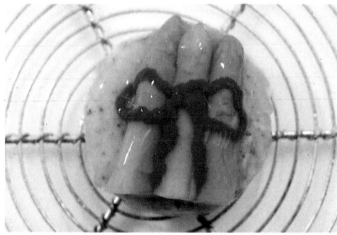

Base

Round canapé of very lightly buttered white bread, spread with a thin coat of herb mayonnaise.

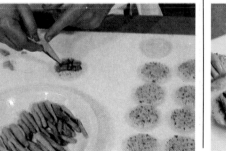

Main Ingredient

Mini green asparagus tips

Assembly

Lay three asparagus tips that are the same length as the diameter of the canapé on the prepared base.

Decoration

Using a paper cone, pipe a ribbon of tomato paste on the asparagus.

Brush on a coat of aspic.

No. 42 Artichoke Bottom Canapés

Base

Round canapé of very lightly buttered white bread, spread with a thin coat of mayonnaise

Main Ingredient

Fresh or canned artichoke bottoms

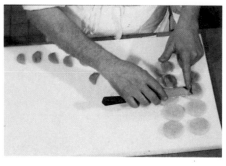

Assembly

Slice the artichoke in thin pieces and arrange them on the prepared canapé.

Decoration

Using a pastry bag fitted with a small star tip, pipe designs with creamed salted butter as shown. Top the rosette with a green peppercorn and decorate with a dot of tomato paste piped from a paper cone.

Brush on a coat of aspic.

No. 43 Broccoli Canapés

Main Ingredient

Steamed broccoli

Assembly

Using a pastry bag fitted with a small star tip, pipe a circle of creamed salted butter to hold the broccoli in place. Set a broccoli floweret on the circle.

Base

Round canapé of olive bread, spread with a thin enough coat of mayonnaise so the olives are still visible.

Decoration

Brush on a coat of aspic.

No. 44 Hearts of Palm Canapés

Base

Round canapé of very lightly buttered white bread, spread with a thin coat of herb mayonnaise

Main Ingredient

Hearts of palm

Assembly

Cut the hearts of palm into 6 mm (1/4 in) slices and lay two slices on the prepared canapé so they are slightly overlapping.

Decoration

Using a pastry bag fitted with a small star tip, pipe a design of creamed salted butter around the slices, as shown. Top the center of the design with a green peppercorn in brine.

Brush on a coat of aspic.

No. 45 Baby Corn Canapés

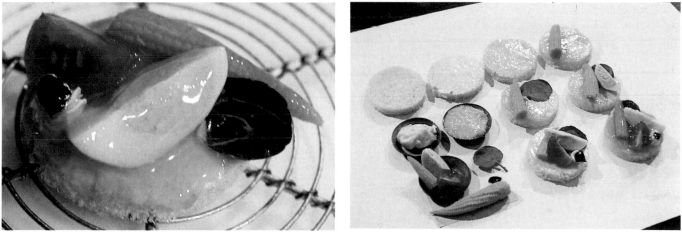

Base

Round canapé of very lightly buttered white bread, spread with a thin coat of mayonnaise.

Main Ingredients

Tiny ears of corn, Watercress, Cherry tomato wedges, Hard-boiled, quartered quail's eggs

Assembly

Place the ingredients on the prepared canapé in an attractive arrangement.

Decoration

Using a pastry bag fitted with a small star tip, pipe a rosette of creamed salted butter on the canapé and top with a piece of black olive.

Brush on a coat of aspic.

No. 46 Mushroom Canapés

Base

Round canapé of very lightly buttered white bread, spread with a thin coat of parsley mayonnaise

Main Ingredient

Cooked mushrooms

Assembly

Trim off the stems and cut the

mushrooms into quarters. Arrange the 4 quarters on the prepared canapé.

Decoration

Using a pastry bag fitted with a small star tip, pipe a rosette of creamed salted butter in the middle of the canapé and top with a sprig of parsley.

Brush on a coat of aspic.

No. 47 Sweet Pepper Canapé

Base

Round canapé of very lightly buttered white bread, spread with a thin coat of mayonnaise.

Main Ingredients

Couscous
Sweet pepper
Raisins
Triangle of lime trimmed of peel and pith
Fresh mint leaves

Assembly

Put a rounded layer of couscous on the prepared canapé and top with a half a sweet pepper, a small mint leaf, a poached raisin and a

small triangle of lime.

Decoration

Brush on a coat of aspic.

No. 48 Canapés with Macédoine of Vegetables

Base

Round canapé of very lightly buttered white bread, spread with a thin coat of mayonnaise

Main Ingredient

Fresh macédoine (cut into small even dice) of vegetables (carrots, turnips, green beans, peas)

Assembly

Using a pastry bag fitted with a small star tip, pipe a heart of creamed salted butter on the prepared canapé, with a rosette at the tip.

Coat the macédoine lightly in aspic to bind it, then fill the heart shape.

Decoration

Using a paper cone, pipe a dot of tomato paste on the rosette.

Brush on a coat of aspic.

No. 49 Comté Canapés

Base

Slice of buttered white bread cut lengthwise from the loaf

Main Ingredient

Slice of Comté cheese cut 3 mm (1/8 in) thick (A flavorful swiss cheese can be used.)

Assembly

Cover the slice of bread with slices of cheese cut to the same size.

Trim the edges of the bread. Cut into squares or rectangles.

Decoration

Using a paper cone, pipe a design in creamed salted butter, as shown.

Brush on a coat of aspic.

Place two sliced toasted almonds on either side of the butter.

No. 50 Roquefort Canapés

Base

Round canapé of walnut bread

Main Ingredients

Roquefort butter (made with 100 g (3 1/2 oz) well-veined Roquefort and 60 g (2 oz) butter)

Assembly

Using a small palette knife, spread the roquefort butter in a slightly rounded layer on the canapé.

Decoration

Sprinkle poppy seeds in a border around the edge of the canapé.

Top the canapé with a walnut half.

No. 51 Parmesan Canapés

Base

Round canapé of very lightly buttered white bread

Main Ingredients

Parmesan sauce
Grated parmesan

Assembly

Using a small palette knife, spread the parmesan sauce in a slightly rounded layer on the canapé.

Sprinkle with the grated cheese.

Decoration

Top with a toasted hazelnut.

No. 52 Gorgonzola Canapés

Base

Round canapé of rye bread

Main Ingredient

Gorgonzola cream (made with 100 g (3 1/2 oz) gorgonzola, 30 g

(1 oz) heavy cream, 30 g (1 oz) butter)

Assembly

Using a small palette knife, spread a slightly rounded layer of gorgonzola cream on the canapé.

Decoration

Lay a slice of pear and a currant on top of the canapé.
Brush on a coat of aspic.

No. 53 Canapés with Munster Cream

Base

Round canapé of very lightly buttered white bread

Main Ingredient

Munster cream (made with 100 g (3 1/2 oz) munster cheese, 30 g (1 oz) heavy cream, 30 g (1 oz) butter).

Assembly

Using a pastry bag fitted with a medium star tip, pipe a rosette of munster cream on the prepared canapé.

Decoration

Sprinkle with cumin seeds.
Brush on a very light coat of aspic.

No. 54 Canapés with "Fromage Frais" and Chives

Base

Round canapé of very lightly buttered white bread

Main Ingredients

"Fromage frais" mousse (made with 200 g (7 oz) "fromage frais" (or cottage cheese passed through a very fine sieve), 60 g (2 oz) heavy cream, 100 g (3 1/2 oz) butter, salt, pepper, snipped chives)

Assembly

Using a pastry bag fitted with a medium star tip, pipe a rosette of cheese mixture on the prepared canapé.

Decoration

Sprinkle with snipped chives. Brush on a very light coat of aspic.

No. 55 Canapés of "Fromage Frais" with Walnuts and Raisins

Base and Main Ingredients
Round canapé of very lightly buttered white bread.

"Fromage frais" mousse (made with 200 g (7 oz) "fromage frais" (or cottage cheese passed through a fine sieve), 60 g (2 oz) heavy cream, 100 g (3 1/2 oz) butter, salt, pepper)

Assembly and Decoration

Using a pastry bag fitted with a medium star tip, pipe a rosette of cheese mixture on the prepared canapé.

Brush on a coat of aspic.

Sprinkle with chopped walnuts. Place a poached currant in the middle of the canapé.

No. 56 Canapés with "Fromage Frais" and Paprika

Base

Round canapé of very lightly buttered white bread

Main Ingredients

"Fromage frais" mousse (made with 200 g (7 oz) "fromage frais" (or cottage cheese passed through a fine sieve), 60 g (2 oz) heavy cream, 100 g (3 1/2 oz) butter, salt, pepper, paprika)

Assembly

Using a pastry bag fitted with a medium star tip, pipe a rosette of cheese mixture on the prepared canapé.

Decoration

Brush on a coat of aspic. Sprinkle with paprika.

No. 57 Mini Goat Cheese Canapés

Base

Round canapé of white bread, brushed with melted butter and toasted

Main Ingredients

Goat cheese cut in small pieces (Small, aged "chevre" is used here, however fresh goat cheese can be used.)
   Watercress
   Salted butter

Assembly

Dip a watercress leaf in aspic and lay it on the prepared canapé.

Using a pastry bag fitted with a small star tip, pipe a rosette of creamed salted butter.

Top with a piece of goat cheese.

Decoration

Lay a quarter of a walnut on either side of the butter rosette.

Aspic Canapés

Presentation

The appearance of aspic canapés is particularly attractive. The crystal clear aspic allows the customer to admire the variety of ingredients that are combined in these canapés.

The color as well as the shape of the ingredients are very important in creating beautiful canapés. The molded aspic is set on a toasted canapé of white bread which makes them easy to handle.

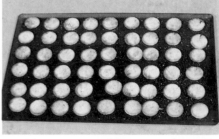

Assembly

Aspic canapés are usually formed in small plastic molds.

Refrigeration is essential in making these canapés.

The canapés are assembled in two layers.

First, pour a little aspic into the mold to cover the bottom.

Refrigerate to set this layer.

Add the prepared garnishes.

Add aspic to just below the rim of the mold.

Chill until set.

Unmolding

Dip the mold into warm water

for a few seconds, then turn it over and unmold the aspic onto the toast that has been previously toasted and cooled.

Storage

Keep the aspic canapés chilled until ready to serve to maintain their fresh appearance and taste.

Serving

At the last moment, remove the aspic canapés from the refrigerator and arrange in neat rows on platters.

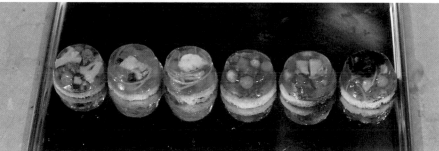

No. 1 Aspic Canapés with Chicken Livers

Chicken livers, seasoned, sautéed in clarified butter then cut into small cubes. Carrots shaped with a small melon baller and dice of zucchini and small flowerets of cauliflower cooked (separately) in boiling salted water or steamed.

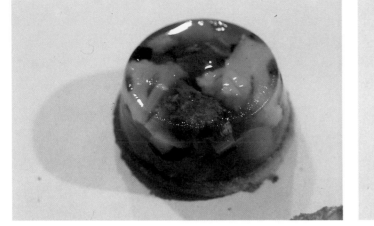

No. 2 Aspic Canapés with Salmon

Small rectangles of fresh poached salmon and salmon eggs. Cucumber shaped with a small melon baller and cooked in boiling salted water or steamed. Lime zest julienned and blanched. Green peppercorns in brine.

**No. 3 Aspic Canapés
with Langoustine**
Shelled langoustine tails that have been poached and cut into pieces. Carrot and cucumber shaped with a small melon baller and cooked (separately) in boiling salted water or steamed. Lime and lemon zest julienned and blanched separately.

**No. 4 Aspic Canapés
with Tongue**
Small strips of tongue. Carrots that have been shaped with a small melon baller, small dice of green beans, peas, cooked (separately) in boiling salted water or steamed.

No. 5 Aspic Canapés with Chicken

Small rectangles of poached chicken breast. Small dice of red pepper, green beans and green peas, cooked (separately) in boiling salted water or steamed.

No. 6 Aspic Canapés with Lumpfish Eggs

Lumpfish eggs. Cucumber shaped with a small melon baller cooked in boiling salted water or steamed. Cooked corn, lime and lemon zest julienned and blanched separately.

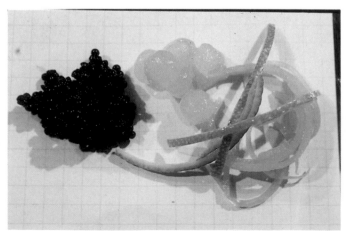

Review of Assembly of the 6 Varieties of Aspic Canapés

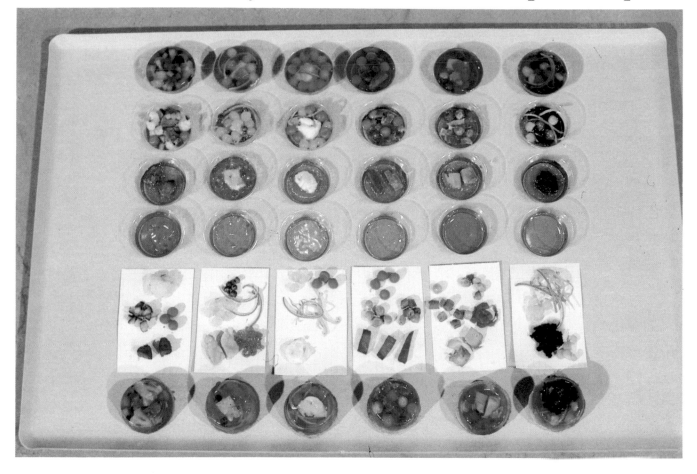

**Use different aspics
to personalize each canapé!**

The flavor of the aspic can highlight the selection of ingredients used in each canapé. Try aspic with port, madeira, sherry or anisette, for example.

Chapter 4
" Mignonnettes " (Assorted Snacks)

∼∼∼∼∼∼∼∼∼∼

Under the heading "mignonnettes" we have grouped a variety of savory hors d'œuvres that complement the selection of canapés. These hors d'œuvres are bite size; some are served hot and others are chilled.

Presentation:

- on a toast or pastry crust base

- served with toothpicks

- as brochettes

Some of these hors d'œuvres are served with a sauce.

These hors d'œuvres round out the selection for a cocktail buffet and can also be served as part of a dinner buffet.

They can also be sold by the piece or by the dozen in a specialty food shop along with other sophisticated and fancy foods.

The 4 Families of " Mignonnettes "

*We have grouped
the " mignonnettes "
in four categories:*

A - Cocktail " Mignonnettes "

These are made with small sausages.

C - " Mignonnettes " made with Fish

Fish and shellfish in different forms.

B - " Mignonnettes " made with Fruits

Fresh and dried fruits.

D - " Mignonnettes " made with Vegetables

Raw and cooked vegetables.

A - Cocktail " Mignonnettes "

7 Varieties of Cocktail " Mignonnettes "

1. **Cocktail Franks**
2. **Spicy Blood Sausages**
3. **Veal Sausages**
4. **Cocktail Franks in Pastry with Mustard**
5. **Veal Sausage on Toasts with Apples**
6. **Spicy Blood Sausage in Pastry with Apple Mousse**
7. **Cocktail Franks with Bacon**

Cocktail Franks in Pastry with Mustard

Ingredients

Tartelette shells made with pâte
   brisée
Mustard
Cocktail franks

Procedure

Blind bake the small tartelette shells. Just before you are ready to serve these hors d'œuvres, warm the baked shells then pipe a little Dijon-style mustard in the bottom of the pastry.

Heat the cocktail franks either by steaming or plunging into gently simmering water (if the water is boiling the franks might burst).

Drain the cocktail franks well on a towel so they do not make the pastry soggy. Place half of a heated cocktail frank in each prepared pastry shell and serve immediately.

Veal Sausage on Toast with Apples

Ingredients

Round toasted slices white bread
Sautéed apple
Veal sausages.

Procedure

Cut rounds of white bread about 3.5 cm (1 1/2in) across and about

6mm (1/4in) thick. Lightly butter the top of the toasts and bake them

in the oven until they are crisp and golden brown.

Preparing the apples

It is preferable to use tart apples for this recipe. Peel the apples and slice them about 3 mm (1/8in) thick then trim them with a pastry cutter that is slightly smaller than the toast.

Sauté the apple slices in clarified butter, turning them carefully with a small spatula to brown them evenly on both sides.

Preparing the sausages

The sausages are also sautéed in clarified butter to brown them on all sides.

Assembly

Just before serving, warm the ingredients. Place an apple slice on the toast then put the sausage on top of the apple.

If the sausages are larger than the toasts they can be cut in half.

Spicy Blood Sausages in Pastry with Apple Mousse

Ingredients

Tartelette shells
Small spicy blood sausages
Apple mousse

Procedure

Blind bake the tartelette shells.

Make a tart apple mousse using very little sugar. Apple sauce in a jar can also be used. Season the mousse with freshly ground pepper and add a little melted butter.

The sausages are sautéed in clarified butter over medium heat so that they don't burst while being heated through.

Assembly

Just before serving, warm the ingredients. Pipe a small amount of apple mousse into the bottom of the pastry, then place the sausage on top.

Presentation

Cocktail "mignonnettes" may be presented

with a single variety on each platter

or

with an assortment of kinds arranged on a large platter.

Cocktail Franks with Bacon

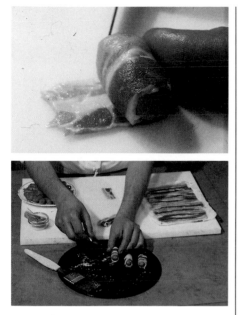

Ingredients

Cocktail franks
Thin slices of smoked bacon

Procedure

If using a slab of bacon, trim the tough outer skin and remove any cartilage. Chill the bacon, which makes it easier to cut thin slices (about 1.5 mm (1/16in). Use an electric slicer if possible for even slices.

Roll the cocktail franks in the slices of bacon, wrapping the bacon around at least 1 1/2 times to allow for shrinkage during cooking. Hold the slice of bacon in place with a toothpick pierced through the sausage.

Cooking

These hors d'œuvres can be cooked two ways:

1. They can be sautéed on top of the stove in clarified butter. Cook them over medium heat, turning them from time to time to brown them evenly.

When the bacon is crisp, drain them on a hand towel or paper towel.

2. They can also be baked in the oven. Put them on a baking sheet brushed with clarified butter, then bake in a hot oven 210 C (400 F). Turn the hors d'œuvres after a few minutes so that they brown evenly.

When the bacon is crisp, remove them from the oven and drain on a towel.

Cocktail franks with bacon are eaten hot and can be served with mustard.

B - " Mignonnettes " made with Fruits

Stuffed Prunes in Bacon

The following recipe is for prunes stuffed with apples. As a variation, almonds or walnuts may be substitued for the apples, using the same techniques.

Banana Slice in Bacon

This is a tasty hors d'œuvre that is easy to make.

Stuffed Prunes in Canadian Bacon

Ingredients

Prunes
Apples (or Walnuts or Almonds)
Butter
Calvados
Canadian Bacon

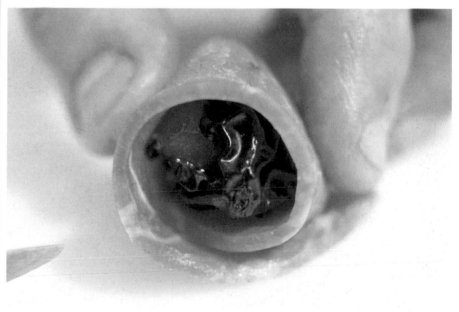

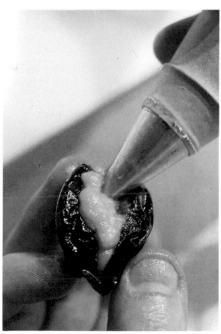

Procedure

It is best to use unpitted prunes. The prunes hold together better when the pits have been removed by hand and they are fresher and more moist.

Preparing the apples

Peel the apples and cut into small rectangles or chunks then trim them to about the size and shape of a garlic clove. Sauté these pieces of apple in clarified butter then flame them with calvados.

The piece of apple can be replaced by apple purée that has been thoroughly cooked to remove excess moisture.

Stuffed Prunes in Canadian Bacon (continued)

Assembly

Slit each prune with a small knife to remove the pit. Fill the pitted prune with the piece of apple. If using the apple purée, pipe a little into the prune with a pastry bag.

The filled prunes are wrapped with Canadian bacon, overlapping the strip of meat and securing it with a toothpick.

Cooking

These hors d'œuvres are always baked in the oven on a buttered baking sheet. When the bacon is crisp, remove them from the oven and drain on a towel.

Banana Slice with Bacon

Ingredients

Banana
Clarified butter
Bacon

Procedure

If using slab bacon, proceed as with cocktail franks with bacon. The bananas are peeled, then cut in slices the same size as the slices of bacon. The slices of banana are then rolled in the bacon overlapping the ends and securing it with a toothpick like the cocktail franks.

Cooking

These hors d'œuvres are always sautéed on top of the stove in clarified butter.

C - " Mignonnettes " made with Fish

Marinated Shrimp

Proportions

250 g (8oz) medium cooked shrimp
1dl (1/2 cup) olive oil
Few drops of Tabasco
6 slices of lemon
(1/2 lemon)
2-3 pinches of dried oregano

Ingredients

Medium cooked shrimp
Olive oil
Slices of lemon
Oregano
Tabasco

Procedure

Remove the shells from the shrimp. Check to make sure there are no remaining bits of shell and place the shrimp in a bowl to marinate.

For the marinade, simply sprinkle the shrimp with olive oil, a little dried oregano and a few drops of Tabasco.

Stir the marinade into the shrimp with a spoon, then place a few slices of lemon on top.

Marinate the shrimp in the refrigerator for at least 2 hours but not more than 2 days.

Presentation

Remove the lemon slices and drain the shrimp in a sieve.
Pierce each shrimp with a toothpick and arrange on plates or in bowls.
Serve chilled.

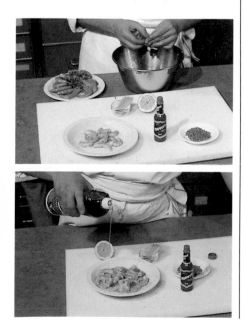

Saltcod fritters

Ingredients

Cream puff pastry made with 1/4 L (1 cup) water, 50 g (1 1/2 oz) butter, 5 g (1tsp) salt, 150 g (5 oz) flour, 3 eggs, pinch black pepper, pinch curry powder, 400 g (14 oz) " brandade de morue " (saltcod purée), made by desalting, boiling, puréeing and enriching the saltcod with olive oil, with added cream, depending on the consistency

Procedure

Make the cream puff pastry, slightly stiff, and stir in the saltcod purée a little at a time.

Using a pastry bag fitted with a plain large tip, pipe out small rounds of the mixture onto a baking sheet.

Cooking

Heat oil in a deep-fryer to 160 C (320 F). Remove the fritters from

the baking sheet using a small palette knife and carefully drop them in the oil.

Fry the fritters until golden brown, turning them from time to

time with a slotted spoon so they color evenly. Remove them with the slotted spoon, drain in a strainer or on a rack for a few seconds, then spread them on paper towel to drain off excess oil.

Presentation

Arrange the fritters in a neat mound on a round platter covered

with a paper doilie. They can be eaten using toothpicks, available on the table. They may be made ahead and reheated in the oven.

" Paupiettes " of Sole in Aspic

Ingredients

Filet of sole
Fish mousse
Fish stock
Aspic made from fish stock and fla-
vored with anise
Lemons - Limes

Fish mousse (for 6 filets of sole)

110 g (3 1/2 oz) filet of pike (or
sole), 1 egg, 100 g (3 1/2 oz heavy
cream), 6 spinach leaves that have
been cooked, squeezed dry and
chopped, 2 tablespoons chopped
herbs (chives, chervil, tarragon)

Purée the pike filets in a food
processor. Add the egg and the
cream and process for a few seconds, then put the mixture through
a fine sieve. In a bowl set over
crushed ice, work the mixture with
a wooden spatula. Season and add
the chopped herbs and the spinach.

Procedure

Season the filets of sole, that
have been flattened lightly with the
flat side of a cleaver. Lay them on
the work surface, skin side up.
Spread a 3 mm (1/8in) layer of fish
mousse on each filet, then roll
them up lengthwise starting with
the narrow end of the filet.

Wrap each " paupiette " in a
piece of plastic film, twisting the
ends of the film tightly to slightly
compress the " paupiette ". Tie the
twisted ends of plastic film with
kitchen twine so they keep their
shape during cooking.

Place the " paupiettes " in cold
fish stock, then bring the temperature up to 80 C (180 F) and poach
for 6 - 8 minutes. Remove from the
heat and leave to cool. Unwrap the
" paupiettes ", then cover them
with a clean hand towel to absorb
the excess moisture.

Assembly

Each paupiette will yield 2 - 3
slices, depending on its size.

Lay the slices on a rack, chill,
then using a soft pastry brush,
apply one coat of the
anise-flavored aspic to make a
smooth surface. On top, arrange a
few strips of lemon and lime zest
that have been cut into fine julienne and blanched. Apply a second
coat of aspic. Put each slice in a
paper case, arrange on a platter and
serve well chilled.

Langoustine Beignets

Ingredients

Langoustines - Deep frying batter - Tartar sauce - Lemon wedges - Oil for frying

Langousting are known as Dublin Boy Prawns in Great Britain, and Salt Water Crayfish in North America.

Procedure

Make the deep frying batter with 500 g (1 lb) flour, 10 g (2 tsp) salt, 4 eggs, 1/2 dl (1/4 cup) beer, 1dl (1/2 cup) oil, 5 beaten egg whites.

Carefully remove the tail meat from the raw langoustines. Rinse them in cold water and dry them with a hand towel.

Dip each langoustine in the batter then drop it carefully into the oil preheated to 160 C (320 F). Turn the fritters as they fry to obtain an even golden color.

Drain on paper towels to absorb excess oil.

Arrange on plates lined with paper doilies and provide toothpicks for easy handling. Garnish with lemon wedges and serve with tartar sauce (for tartar sauce recipe, see Broccoli Fritters).

Serve immediately. These fritters do not reheat well.

Monkfish Fritters

Ingredients

Monkfish
Marinade made with lemon slices, fresh or dried thyme, bay leaf, salt, pepper, anisette
Deep frying batter (see Langoustine Fritters)
Oil for frying
Tartar sauce
Lemon wedges

Procedure

Cut small slices of monkfish about 1.5 cm (1/2in) thick and put them in a bowl to marinate.

Season with salt and pepper, sprinkle with a few drops of anisette and place the branches of

thyme, bay leaf and lemon slices on top and, marinate for at least one hour.

Cooking

Remove the lemon slices, thyme and bay leaf and with a fork dip

each piece of monkfish in the batter and proceed as with langoustine fritters.

The monkfish fritters are presented in the same manner as the langoustine fritters.

D - Mignonnettes made with Vegetables
Broccoli Fritters

Ingredients

Broccoli
Deep frying batter
Oil for frying
Tartar sauce

Procedure

Separate the broccoli into small flowerets and wash them carefully in cold water. Drain them in a sieve.

Steam the broccoli over a pot of boiling water. The broccoli should remain crunchy as it will be cooked again when it is fried.

Frying

Dry the cooked broccoli on a hand towel, season the flowerets with salt and pepper. Dip them into the deep frying batter then drop them into the heated oil.

The frying procedure and the presentation is the same as with the other fritters in this chapter.

Tartar Sauce

Ingredients

a) *Mayonnaise*
2 egg yolks
1 tbsp Dijon style mustard
Salt
Cayenne pepper

1/2 L (2 cups) oil (corn or peanut)
A few drops of vinegar

b) *Flavorings*
100 g (3 1/2 oz) onions
60 g (2 oz) capers
60 g (2 oz) cornichons
(or other tart pickle)
30 g (1 oz) parsley.

Procedure

Make a stiff mayonnaise.
Prepare the garnish: Peel and cut the onion in fine dice. Drain the capers. Drain the cornichons then chop them finely. Trim the parsley, wash it and dry it thoroughly. Chop the parsley very finely with a chef's knife.
Stir in the prepared garnish and check for seasoning.

Presentation

Serve the tartar sauce in a bowl to accompany fritters and other complementary dishes such as seafood.

Celery Sticks with Roquefort

Ingredients

Celery sticks
Roquefort butter
Walnut halves

Procedure

Trim the stem and leaves from a bunch of celery, wash the stalks thoroughly and dry them on a clean hand towel.

Cut the stalks into small sticks about 5 cm (2in) long. Some parts of the stalks will have a better hollow shape to hold the roquefort butter.

Choose these parts for the hors d'œuvres and keep the rest of the celery for another use.

Trim the tough strings from the outside of the stalks with a vegetable peeler.

Make a roquefort butter with 4 parts roquefort and 1 part butter. Choose roquefort that has a large percentage of the flavorful mold throughout.

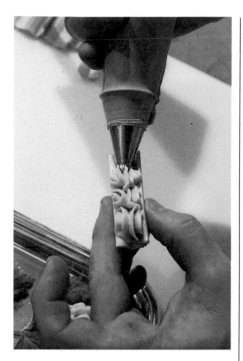

Use a pastry bag fitted with a star tip to pipe the roquefort butter into the hollow of the celery sticks. Garnish with a walnut half cut in half lengthwise.

Arrange on platters using the celery leaves to decorate.

Pass these ingredients through a fine-meshed sieve then blend until smooth.

Belgian Endive Leaves
with Smoked Salmon or Foie Gras

Endive with Salmon

Ingredients

Endive leaves
Sour cream
Smoked salmon
Fish aspic
Dill

Endive with Foie Gras

Ingredients

Endive leaves
Purée of foie gras
Truffle
Aspic flavored with port

Preparing the endive

Choose firm, fresh endive. Separate the leaves and set aside the large ones to make these hors d'œuvres and use the remaining leaves in salad.

Wash the leaves in cold water and dry them on a clean hand towel taking care not to crush the leaves.

Procedure

For the endive with salmon

Season the sour cream with salt and pepper.

Pipe about 1/2 teaspoon of cream into each endive leaf then

place a thin slice of salmon on top.

Chill the hors d'œuvres then brush them with a thin coat of fish aspic and garnish the top with a sprig of dill.

For the endive with foie gras

Stir the purée of foie gras to a creamy consistency.

Using a pastry bag fitted with a star tip, pipe the foie gras into the hollow of the leaves of endive.

Place a small piece of truffle in the center of each hors d'œuvre.

Chill thoroughly, then brush on a thin layer of port-flavored aspic with a soft pastry brush.

Presentation

Arrange in neat rows on platters and serve well chilled.

Stuffed Grape Leaves

Ingredients

Grape leaves
Cooked rice
Olive oil
Anchovies
Tuna packed in oil
Parsley
Onions
Greek olives
Lemon
Salt and pepper

Grape Leaf Stuffing

100 g (3 1/2 oz) cooked rice
10 anchovy filets
100 g (3 1/2oz) tuna packed in oil
10 Greek olives
45 g (1 1/2 oz) onions
1 tablespoon chopped parsley
2.5 cl (1/8 cup) olive oil
A few drops lemon juice
Ground pepper and salt

Procedure

Grape leaves are purchased blanched, packed in brine in glass jars. They are usually available in specialty food shops.

Chop the anchovies. Mash the tuna with a fork. Pit the olives and cut them in small dice. Cut the onion in small dice.

Drain the rice well. Place it in a bowl and add the prepared ingredients and blend well. Season with olive oil, lemon juice and salt and pepper. Stir in the chopped parsley. Check the seasoning.

Filling

Drain the grape leaves on a hand towel.
Cut the leaves in two (if they are large) and lay them out with the veins of the leaf up.

Place a teaspoon of the filling in the center of each leaf.

To roll the leaf around the filling, first overlap two ends over the filling then roll the leaf tightly.

Place the stuffed leaves in a single layer in a dish to marinate. Sprinkle the leaves with a little olive oil and a few drops of lemon juice.

Cover the dish with plastic wrap and marinate them in the refrigerator for at least 48 hours.

When ready to serve the stuffed grape leaves, transfer them carefully to a rack to drain, then arrange them in even rows on platters. Serve with toothpicks.

These hors d'œuvres are eaten at room temperature.

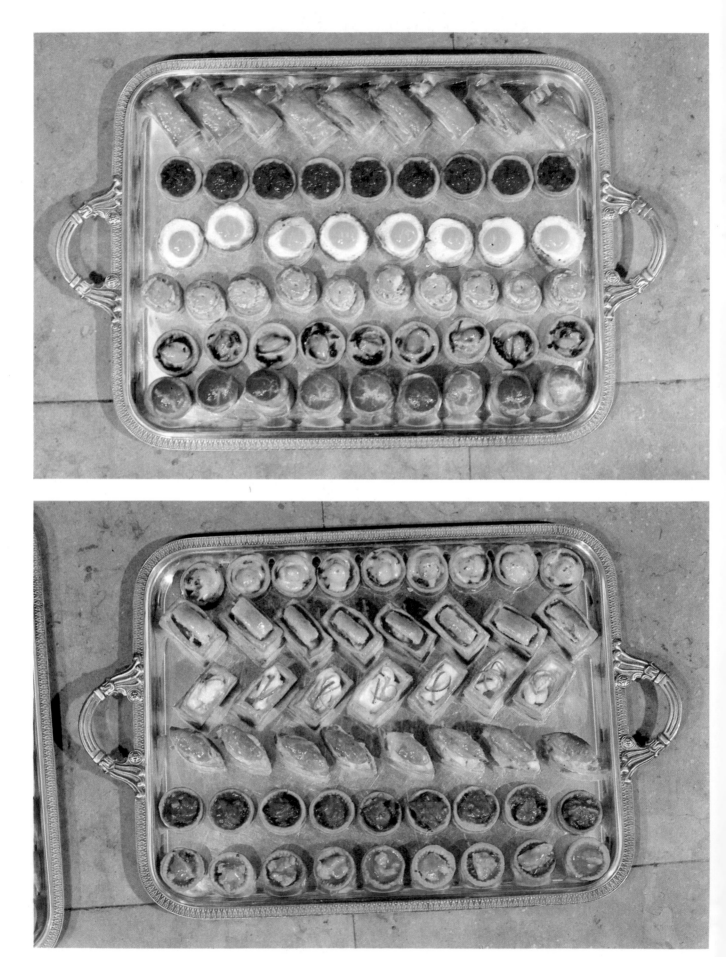

Chapter 5
Hot Hors d'Œuvres

These bite-size hors d'œuvres add a touch of elegance to a cocktail buffet or dinner menu.

They are made in two steps. First, a base of pastry or toasted bread is shaped and baked, then a filling is prepared separately.

These hors d'œuvres are then assembled at the last minute and served hot.

Several of the fillings are accompanied by a sauce, which enhances the flavor, keeps the filling moist and gives these hors d'œuvres a shiny appearance.

These lovely snacks are often served as "finger food" at a stand-up buffet and can also accompany an aperitif before a sit-down dinner.

131

Hot Hors d'Œuvres

Introduction

Pictured above are the 12 hot hors d'œuvres that are described in this chapter (from top left, clockwise).

1. "Feuilletés" with Asparagus Tips
2. "Croustades" with Sweet Pepper Compote
3. Quail Eggs on Toast
4. Snail "Bouchées"
5. "Croustades" of Mussels with Curry Sauce
6. Mini-Brioches with Crab
7. "Croustades" of Sweetbreads with Sherry Sauce
8. "Croustades" of Chicken Livers with Raspberry Vinegar Sauce
9. Mini "Bouchées à la Reine"
10. "Feuilletés" with Sole and Lime
11. "Feuilletés" with Prawns
12. "Croustades" of Bay Scallops with Chervil Sauce

Storage

Since these hors d'œuvres are composed of a pastry or crouton base with a moist filling, they do not keep well after they are filled. For the best results, the different components are prepared in advance, heated separately, then assembled and served immediately. Alternatively, they can be assembled in advance, then warmed through just before serving.

The Pastry Bases for Hot Hors d'œuvres

1. Puff Pastry bases

For maximum flavor and lightness it is best to use puff pastry made with butter only. Although puff pastry with trimmings (see pp. 8-9) can be used, puff pastry made with no trimmings added is recommended because it usually rises a little higher and more evenly.

The shapes in this chapter include the classic round and rectangular shapes as well as oval. The difference in shape not only helps to distinguish one filling from another, but makes a very decorative arrangement on a platter.

Three of the puff pastry bases in this chapter are cut from a single sheet of dough, rolled out to 5 mm (about 1/4 in). The shapes are either scored before baking, which creates a "lid" in the finished pastry or else the shape is split in two after baking. The other puff pastry cases are made from two sheets of dough rolled out to about 3 mm (1/8 in). Rectangles are shaped for the bottom, then a second rectangle is made with the center removed with a smaller pastry cutter, leaving a border. The bottom is then brushed with egg glaze, then the border is carefully placed on top. The method creates cases that have a deep hollow center and therefore can easily hold a sauce.

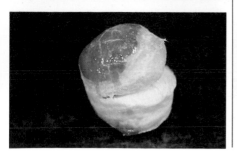

2. Pie Pastry bases

The "croustades" (small pie shells) in this chapter are made with a base of basic pie pastry (pâte brisée) which is pressed into small round molds, then baked and filled.

The pastry, which is pricked with a roller-docker, is pressed into the molds by hand. The croustades are chilled, then weights are placed in each lined mold to prevent the pastry from puffing during baking. ("Muffin" papers work well as containers for the weights.)

3. Toasted Bread bases

Use pain de mie (milk-enriched white bread) or pain brioché (egg-enriched, but less rich than classic brioche) to make the toasted bread bases. The example in this chapter is cut in a round to match the size and shape of the quail egg.

For other toppings without sauce, the bread can be cut in rectangles, squares or triangles.

The bread

The bread is sliced 8-10 mm (about 3/8 in) thick, shaped by hand with a serrated knife or with a pastry cutter, then the bases are usually brushed with melted butter on one side before being toasted on sheet pans in the oven until crisp and golden brown.

4. Brioche bases

The mini-brioche pictured here is made like the small rolls in the previous chapter (see p. 52). The dough is chilled, which makes it stiff enough to be rolled out. The small round shapes are cut from a sheet of dough 6 mm (1/4 in) thick. The shapes rise until doubled, then are brushed with egg glaze, and then bake in a hot oven (210 C (400 F)). An average size is 10 g (1/3oz) raw dough per brioche.

These small brioches bake quickly. The baked brioches need to be cooled completely (even refrigerated) in order to cut them open neatly. They can be made in advance and frozen in containers with tight lids until needed.

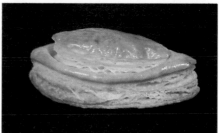

1. "Feuilletés" with Asparagus Tips

Ingredients

Puff pastry bases
Asparagus tips
"Beurre blanc"

Preparing of Asparagus Tips

Choose medium size green asparagus and cut off the tips about 5 cm (2 in) long.

Bring lightly salted water to a full boil in a large pot. Plunge the asparagus into the boiling water and cook until tender but firm.

Remove immediately and plunge

the cooked asparagus into a bowl of ice water to stop the cooking. As soon as they are cool, drain on a hand towel and set aside.

Making the Puff Pastry Bases

Roll out a sheet of puff pastry to about 6 mm (1/4 in) then cut into

even rectangles 6.5 cm (2 1/2 in) long and 2.5 cm (1 in) wide.

Brush with egg glaze. Prick each shape in an even north-south-east-west pattern to create small air vents to help the pastry rise evenly.

Place the shapes to rest in the refrigerator for one hour before baking at 210 C (400 F). After baking, set aside to cool completely.

Making the "Beurre Blanc"

Beurre blanc is a delicate butter-based sauce that marries well with vegetables.

20 g (2/3oz) clarified butter
80 g (2 1/2oz) shallots (2)
5 cl (1/4 cup) dry white wine
5 cl (1/4 cup) wine vinegar
3 cl (2 tbsp) heavy cream
200 g (7oz) cold butter

Cut the shallots into very fine dice and put them in a saucepan with the clarified butter. Cook the shallots gently until soft but not brown. Add the wine and vinegar and reduce by 1/3.

Add the heavy cream and bring to a boil.

Lower the heat to a simmer, then cut the cold butter into small pieces and incorporate a few pieces at a time, stirring constantly with a wooden spatula or whisk until completely melted.

Season to taste with salt and pepper. Pass the sauce through a fine-meshed conical strainer, pressing on the shallots to extract all the flavor.

Assembly

Carefully slice off the top 1/3 of each feuilleté with a paring knife.

Also with the paring knife, pierce an asparagus tip as shown and dip it in the sauce, then slide it off the knife onto the bottom of the feuilleté.

Place the top of the pastry on the asparagus.

Arrange on a platter and keep warm until ready to serve.

2. *"Croustades"*
with Sweet Pepper Compote

Ingredients

Small pie shells (croustades) made with basic pie pastry
Sweet pepper compote

Making the Croustades

Roll out basic pie pastry to about 3 mm (1/8 in), cut out shapes that correspond to the shape and size of the mold you are using (round or boat-shaped) and gently press the pastry into the molds.

Put the lined molds in the refrigerator to rest for at least two hours,

then blind bake the pastry shells with weights at 210 C (400 F) until thoroughly baked.

Making the Sweet Pepper Compote

Use red and green (or yellow) peppers to make this compote. Cut them in half, remove the seeds and

the white membranes from inside and cut into small dice.

Place the diced peppers in a sauté pan with a little olive oil (about 2.5 cl (1/8 cup) per pepper), and cook gently over medium heat until tender but still firm (about 10 mn).

Salt to taste. Stir in a little thick tomato sauce (coulis) to bind the peppers.

Taste again for seasoning.

Assembly

Reheat the baked shells and fill them to the rim with warm compote and serve immediately.

If you wish to assemble them ahead of time, cool the compote first, fill the cooled shells, then reheat at the last moment.

These croustades are also good eaten at room temperature.

3. Toast Rounds with Quail Eggs

Ingredients

Toast rounds made with "pain de mie" (enriched white bread)
Liver mousse
Quail eggs
Clarified butter

Making the Croutons

Slice the bread 1 cm (3/8 in) thick, then cut out 5 cm (2 in) rounds.

Brush the rounds with melted butter, place them on a baking sheet and toast in the oven at 210 C (400 F) 6-8 minutes until golden brown and crisp.

Preparing the Mousse

If using prepared liver mousse (mousse de foie), whisk it to a spreadable consistency.

A purée of sauté chicken livers, creamed with butter could also be used.

Preparing the Quail Eggs

The shells of the quail eggs are quite tough, so to avoid breaking the yolk when cracking the eggs, use a paring knife to crack them open. It is best to first break them one at a time into a small bowl and then carefully transfer them to a frying pan in which a little clarified butter has been heated.

Cook over moderate heat until the whites are cooked through and the yolks are just "set".

Use a small flexible palette knife to remove the cooked eggs to a cutting board. Trim the white with the same pastry cutter used to cut the toast rounds.

Assembly

Spread each toast round with a thin layer of the liver mousse.

Set a warm, trimmed egg on top, arrange on platters and serve immediately.

4. "Bouchées" with Snails

Ingredients

"Bouchées" (bite sized rounds of puff pastry)
Snails (available in cans)
"Snail butter"

Making the Bouchées

Roll the puff pastry to a thickness of 6 mm (1/4 in) and cut out rounds with a pastry cutter measuring 5 cm (2 in).

Place the rounds of dough in even rows on a moistened baking sheet.

Brush the top with egg glaze taking care not to drip any glaze on the sides which would inhibit the pastry from rising.

To achieve neat little "lids" on each bouchée, dip a smaller round pastry cutter (2.5 cm (1 in)) in hot oil and score the center of each round of pastry.

Prick each shape in an even north-south-east-west pattern to create small air vents to help the

pastry rise evenly. Place the shapes to rest in the refrigerator for one hour before baking.

Bake at 210 C (400 F) until evenly browned. After they are baked, lift off the "lid" with a paring knife. Set aside to cool completely.

Preparing the Snails

Drain the snails in a sieve and set aside.

The preparation of fresh snails is quite lengthy and is explained in detail in Volume 2 of this series.

Assembly

Place a drained snail in the bottom of each "bouchée". Using a pastry bag and a small star tip, pipe a rosette of snail butter on top of each snail. Place the lid on top of the butter.

Presentation

These hors d'œuvre can be prepared a few hours in advance and reheated at the last minute.

Reheat in a moderate oven so that the hors d'œuvre warm through without losing all the delicious snail butter.

Making the Snail Butter

30 g (1 oz) Italian parsley - 10 g (1/3 oz) shallots - 15 g (1/2 oz) garlic - Salt, pepper, nutmeg - Few drops anisette - 250 g (8 oz) butter

Chop the parsley and garlic very finely. Cut the shallots into very fine dice. Cream the butter and stir in the prepared ingredients. Season with salt and pepper, a little nutmeg and a few drops of anisette. Blend well.

5. "Croustades" with Curried Mussels

Ingredients

Small shells (croustades) made with basic pie pastry
Spinach
Mussels
Curry sauce

Preparing the Croustades

Prepare the small croustades following the instructions on p. 136.

Preparing the Mussels

Scrape the shells of the mussels with a paring knife to remove seaweed, barnacles and sand. Rinse in several changes of cold water to clean them thoroughly.

Steam them open "à la marinière", using the following ingredients.

Butter, onions, shallots, bouquet garni, white wine, freshly ground pepper

When the mussels have opened, drain them in a large sieve, reserving the cooking liquid for the curry sauce.

Remove the mussels from their shells and pull off the dark rim or "beard".

Assembly

Fill the bottom of the croustades with the cooked spinach. Place one mussel (or two small) on the spinach, then cover with a spoonful of curry sauce.

Warm gently before serving.

Preparing the Spinach

Remove the stems from the spinach and clean thoroughly in cold water.

Steam the spinach, then drain.

Chop coarsely then sauté in butter that has been heated until it turns light brown and smells "nutty". Evaporate any water that is left in the spinach.

Season with salt and pepper and nutmeg to taste and set aside.

Preparing the Curry Sauce

Pass the cooking juices from the mussels through a fine-meshed conical sieve. Bring to a boil and whisk in enough cooked roux to thicken slightly. Enrich the sauce with a little heavy cream and season with curry powder.

Simmer the sauce briefly to achieve a homogeneous, velvety texture. Finish the sauce by whisking in a few small pieces of butter.

6. Mini-Brioches with Crab

Ingredients

Mini-brioches
Crab
Sauce Nantua

Preparing the Mini Brioches

Take a chilled portion of brioche dough and roll out into a sheet 8-10 mm (about 3/8 in) thick.

Cut out small rounds with a pastry cutter approximately 4 cm (1 3/4 in) across. (For more details about shaping brioche, see p. 133.)

Place the rounds of dough in even rows on a moistened baking

sheet. Brush once with egg glaze, then leave them to rise in a warm place until double their height. Brush on a second layer of egg glaze and bake at 210 C (400 F).

Preparing the Crab

Drain the crab (if using canned crab) and flake it apart. Remove all bits of shell. Keep refrigerated until ready to use.

Preparing the Nantua Sauce

Place 2 dl (3/4 cup) of "sauce américaine" and 1/2 L (2 cups) of fish stock in a saucepan and reduce by half. Skim any impurities that accumulate on the surface.

Whisk in a little cooked roux to thicken slightly. Pass the sauce through a fine-meshed conical sieve.

Add a little (1dl (1/3 cup)) heavy cream. Simmer the sauce briefly to achieve a homogeneous, velvety texture. Season to taste with salt, pepper and cayenne. Finish the sauce with a little crayfish butter and a drop of cognac.

Assembly

Cut off the top 1/2 of each brioche and trim the top with the 4 cm (1 3/4 in) pastry cutter.

Hollow out the bottom with a paring knife. The interior removed can be made into delicious breadcrumbs for another dish.

Mix the drained crab with the Nantua sauce. Fill each mini-brioche with a spoonful of the crab mixture, mounding the mixture slightly above the rim.

Place a top on each brioche and reheat in a moderate oven before serving.

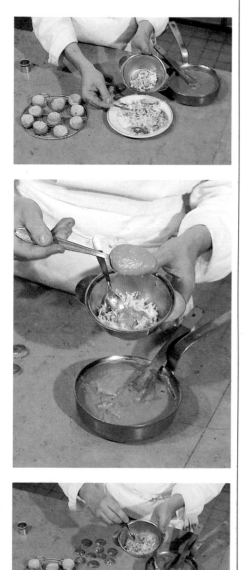

7. "Croustades" of Bay Scallops with Chervil Sauce

Ingredients

Pastry shells (croustades) made with basic pie pastry
Mushroom duxelles
Bay scallops
Chervil sauce

Making the Croustades

See page 133.

Making the Mushroom Duxelles

60 g (2 oz) shallots
200 g (7 oz) mushrooms
30 g (1 oz) clarified butter
Salt and pepper

Cut the shallots into very fine dice and cook in clarified butter until tender but not brown. Wash the mushrooms thoroughly, rub them with lemon and chop finely with a chef's knife.

Add the mushrooms to the cooked shallots and season with a little salt and freshly ground pepper. Cover and cook over medium high heat to draw out the moisture from the mushrooms.

Uncover and cook over medium heat, stirring often until the mushrooms are cooked and the liquid has evaporated.

Preparing the Bay Scallops

Place the scallops in a small pot, cover with fish stock and poach gently.

The small scallops will cook very quickly; as soon as they are firm to the touch, remove and drain. Reserve the fish stock for the sauce.

Preparing the Chervil Sauce

20 g (2/3 oz) clarified butter
2 shallots
45 g (1 1/2 oz) mushrooms (stems and peelings)
10 sprigs chervil
7 cl (1/3 cup) white wine
7 cl (1/3 cup) dry vermouth
1/4 L (1 cup) fish stock
1/2 L (2 cups) heavy cream
salt, pepper
60 g (2 oz) cold butter

Cut the shallots into fine dice, chop the mushrooms finely and sauté in the clarified butter until tender but not brown. Add the white wine and bring to a boil for 2 minutes. Add the vermouth and reduce slightly. Add the fish stock and reduce by half.

Whisk in enough cooked roux to thicken slightly.

Add the heavy cream and simmer to reduce slightly. Taste to season.

Pass the sauce through a conical sieve, then finish with a little butter.

Assembly

Fill the bottom of the croustades with a spoonful of mushroom duxelles. Place a drained scallop on top.

Cover the scallops with a spoonful of sauce and garnish with a sprig of chervil. Serve warm.

8. "Feuilletés" with Prawns

Ingredients
Small rectangular cases of puff pastry (feuilletés)
Vegetable "mirepoix"
Prawns
Sauce "américaine"

Making the Puff Pastry Cases
Roll out a sheet of puff pastry to 3 mm (1/8 in) and cut into even rectangles, 6 cm (about 2 1/2 in) long and 3 cm (1 1/2 in) wide. Half of the rectangles will serve as the bottom of the case; the rest form the tops and are cut out to form a rectangular border, as shown below.

Place the full rectangles in even rows on a baking sheet and brush

with egg glaze. Carefully place the rectangular rims on top, pressing down very gently to stick the two layers together. Brush egg glaze on the rim, and prick on each side. Place the shapes to rest in the re-

frigerator for one hour before cooking.

Bake at 210 C (400 F) until evenly brown. With a paring knife, trim out the middle of each rectangle which will serve as the lid of the case.

Making the Vegetable "Mirepoix"
20 g (about 1 1/2 tsp) clarified butter - 40 g (1 1/2 g oz) shallots - 150 g (5 oz) carrots - 50 g (about 2 oz) onion - 100 g (3 1/2 oz) fennel - salt, pepper

Wash and peel the vegetables. Cut them into very fine dice (mirepoix).

Heat the clarified butter over medium heat, stir in the vegetables and cover with a tight-fitting lid.

Stir the vegetables after a few minutes. Continue cooking until they are tender, yet firm.

Season the mirepoix with a little salt and pepper.

The mirepoix can be made in advance and kept until the hors d'œuvres are ready to be assembled.

Preparing the Prawns

Remove the shell from the raw prawn by twisting the head from the tail, then carefully pulling the shell off the tail.

Rinse the tail meat and remove the dark "vein" that is found on each tail.

Poach the tail meat in fish stock until just firm to the touch. Drain on a hand towel.

Preparing the Sauce "Américaine"

Start with a full-flavored sauce "américaine". If the flavor is not pronounced, reduce the sauce until the flavor is more concentrated.

Whisk in a little cooked roux to thicken the sauce slightly. Add a little heavy cream (5 cl (1/4 cup)), taste for seasoning, then finish with a few drops of cognac.

Pass the sauce through a fine-meshed conical sieve and set aside.

Assembly

Fill the bottom of each puff pastry case with the cooked mirepoix of vegetables. Place a poached prawn on top of the vegetables. Cover the prawns with a spoonful of sauce "américaine" and place the "lid" of pastry on top.

Reheat gently before serving.

NOTE: If serving the hors d'œuvres immediately, the "feuilleté" can be warmed in the oven, then vegetables and prawns warmed up separately and the fresh hot sauce spooned over at the last minute.

9. "Feuilletés" of Sole with Lime

Ingredients

Puff pastry cases (feuilletés)
Filets of sole
Lime sections trimmed of peel and pith
Julienne of lime zest
Sauce

Making the Puff Pastry Cases

Roll out a sheet of puff pastry to 3 mm (1/8 in) and cut into even rectangles, 6 cm (about 2 1/2 in) long and 3 cm (1 1/2 in) wide.

Half of the rectangles will serve as the bottom of the case; the rest form the tops and are cut out to form a rectangular border, as shown below.

Place the full rectangles in even rows on a baking sheet and brush with egg glaze. Carefully place the rectangular rims on top, pressing down very gently to stick the two layers together.

Brush egg glaze on the rim, and prick on each side. Place the shapes to rest in the refrigerator for one hour before cooking.

Bake at 210 C (400 F) until evenly brown. With a paring knife, trim out the middle of each rectangle which will serve as the lid of the case.

Preparing the Lime

Wash the limes well.

Cut off the ends of the lime, then with a vegetable peeler, remove the zest. To make large pieces of zest that will result in even julienne, hold the lime firmly and peel from one end to the other.

Remove as little of the white pith as possible. Cut the pieces of zest into fine julienne with a chef's knife.

Blanch the julienne of zest by placing it in a small pot of cold water and bringing it to a boil and cook for about 4 minutes.

Drain the julienne in a strainer and rinse with cold water. Repeat the blanching process to obtain zest that is soft and not bitter.

Using a flexible stainless steel knife, remove the white pith that remains on the limes.

Cut between the sections to remove the flesh in neat segments.

Preparing the "Goujonnettes"

Cut the filets of sole into small strips (about 5 cm x 1.5 cm (2 in x

1/2 in)) at a diagonal across the "grain".

Sauté the strips (goujonnettes) in hot butter. They will cook very quickly (about 2 minutes). Season with a little salt, freshly ground pepper and a few drops of lime juice.

Remove the cooked goujonnettes to a plate until ready to assemble the hors d'œuvres.

Making the Sauce

In a saucepan, reduce 5 cl (1/4 cup) of lime juice by 9/10, or until the juice becomes very thick and syrupy.

Add 1/4 L (1cup) heavy cream and reduce by half.

Over low heat, whisk in 100 g (3 1/2 oz) butter. Season to taste.

Pass the sauce through a fine-meshed conical sieve. Set aside.

Assembly

Place a cooked goujonnette of sole at one end of each pastry case and a segment of lime at the other. Cover this filling with a spoonful of sauce, taking care not to drip sauce on the sides of the pastry case. Garnish with the blanched lime zest. Serve warm.

10. Mini "Bouchées à la Reine"

Ingredients

Small oval or round bases of puff pastry (bouchées)

Chicken and sweetbread filling "à la reine"

Making the Puff Pastry Bases

Roll out a sheet of puff pastry to 6 mm (1/4 in) and using an oval pastry cutter, stamp out the bouchées.

Place the rounds of dough in even rows on a moistened baking sheet.

Brush the top with egg glaze taking care not to drip any glaze on the sides which would inhibit the pastry from rising.

To form neat little "lids" on each bouchée, score a border in the pastry with the tip of a sharp knife, or dip a smaller pastry cutter in hot oil and score the center of each round of pastry.

Prick each shape in an even north-south-east-west pattern to create small air vents to help the pastry rise more evenly. Place the shapes to rest in the refrigerator for one hour before baking.

Bake at 210 C (400 F) until evenly brown. After they are baked, lift off the "lid" with a paring knife. Set aside to cool completely.

Preparing the Chicken and Sweetbread Filling

This classic filling, "fit for a queen" ("à la reine") is used to fill larger pastries served as a first course as well as these delicious hors d'œuvres.

The traditional ingredients are:

Braised sweetbreads

Veal or chicken quenelles

Poached brains (additional sweetbreads or quenelles can replace brains if they are not available)

Cooked mushrooms

If you are making the filling to be used in both large and small pastries, cut the meats in larger pieces, put aside enough cooked filling for these hors d'œuvres and chop it a little to make it easier to spoon into

Assembly

Use a teaspoon to fill the feuilletés with the prepared mixture, mounding the filling amply above the rim. Place a lid on top of each hors d'oeuvre.

Presentation

To heat the hors d'œuvres, place them in a warm oven (180 C (350 F)) for about 4 minutes. Arrange on platters and serve warm.

the bite size pastries.

If making the filling specifically for these hors d'œuvres, cut all of the ingredients smaller to begin with.

A velouté sauce made with a light roux and veal or chicken stock is combined with the above ingredients.

The cooking juices from the sweetbreads and mushrooms are reduced and added to the sauce. This sauce is enriched and bound at the end with egg yolks and heavy cream.

Taste for seasoning and pass the sauce through a fine-meshed conical sieve.

Combine the sauce and the prepared meats and mushrooms and chill until ready to assemble the hors d'œuvres.

11. "Croustades" of Chicken Livers

Ingredients

Small pastry shells (croustades) made of basic pie pastry

Cooked spinach - Sautéed chicken livers - Raspberry vinegar sauce

Making the Croustades

Roll out basic pie pastry to about 3 mm (1/8 in), cut out shapes that correspond to the shape and size of mold you are using (round or boat-shaped) and gently press the pastry into the molds. Put the lined molds in the refrigerator to rest for at least two hours, then blind bake the pastry shells with weights at 210 C (400 F) until thoroughly baked.

Preparing the Spinach

Remove the stems from the spinach and clean thoroughly in cold water. The spinach is cooked in

two stages. First, the leaves are softened by placing them in a large pot with a little clarified butter.

Cover with a tight-fitting lid and cook over a high heat, stirring the spinach from time to time with a long-tined fork. Large quantities of spinach (1.5-2 kg (3-4 lb)) will take about 4-5 minutes to "cook down".

Drain the spinach in a strainer

and chop coarsely. To evaporate the liquid that is still held in the leaves (so the croustades will not get soggy) it is necessary to cook the spinach a second time.

In a pan, heat butter (about 60 g (2 oz) for 1.5-2 kg (3-4 lb)) until it turns light brown and smells "nutty". Add the spinach and cook over medium heat, stirring with the long-tined fork so that the spinach does not stick to the pan.

When there is no more liquid, season to taste. Remove the spinach to a plate, and set aside.

Preparing the Chicken Livers

Thoroughly trim the chicken livers, removing all fat, filaments and discolored parts. Salt and pepper the livers, tossing them to coat

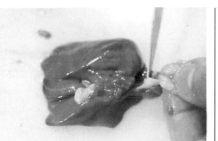

them evenly with the seasoning.

For each 500 g (1 lb) of trimmed livers, use 45 g (1 1/2 oz) clarified butter. Heat the butter in a pan large enough to accommodate the livers in a single layer. Add the livers to the hot butter and sauté them over a high heat, turning them frequently with a wooden

spatula or palette knife. After a minute, add 75 g (2 1/2 oz) finely diced shallots and cook until the shallots are soft but not brown. The livers should remain slightly pink inside. Remove and set aside. Reserve the pan to make the sauce.

Making the Sauce
Pour off the fat left from cooking the livers, reserving the shallots.

Deglaze the pan with 6 cl (1/4 cup) of raspberry vinegar. Reduce by 3/4. Add 1/2 L (2 cups) of demi-glace (reduced meat stock) and reduce by 1/2. Whisk in enough cooked roux to achieve a sauce with a smooth,

velvety texture that will coat a spoon. Taste for seasoning. Pass the sauce through a fine-meshed conical sieve into a saucepan, pressing down

on the shallots with a small ladle to extract all the flavor.

Finish the sauce by whisking in about 30 g (1 oz) of cold butter, a little at a time.

Assembly
Place a spoonful of cooked spin-

ach in the bottom of each croustade. Cut the chicken livers into pieces that will fit neatly in the pastry shells and place a piece on top of the spinach.

Cover the liver with a spoonful of the sauce.

Heat the hors d'œuvres in a warm oven for a few minutes, arrange on platters and serve immediately.

12. "Croustades" with Sweetbreads

Ingredients

Small pastry shells (croustades) made with basic pie pastry
Mushroom duxelles
Braised sweetbreads
Sherry vinegar sauce

Making the Croustades

Roll out basic pie pastry to about 3 mm (1/8 in), cut out shapes that correspond to the shape and size of mold you are using (round or boat-shaped) and gently press the pastry into the molds.

Put the lined molds in the refrigerator to rest for at least two hours, then blind bake the pastry shells with weights at 210 C (400 F) until thoroughly baked.

Making the Mushroom Duxelles
Same as p. 146

Braising the Sweetbreads
Trim the sweetbreads, removing the thin skin that covers them. Degorge the trimmed sweetbreads in cold water to draw out any blood. Drain on a hand towel.

To braise 500 g (1 lb) trimmed sweetbreads, use the following ingredients:

60 g (2 oz) carrots, 45 g (1 1/2 oz) onions, 20 g (2/3 oz) shallots, 30 g (1 oz) celery, 45 g (1 1/2 oz) leek (white part only), 1 bouquet garni

(parsley stems, sprig of thyme, piece of bay leaf, leek green)

Heat 45 g (1 1/2 oz) clarified butter in a low, straight-sided pan that fits in the oven with a tight-fitting lid. Lightly brown the sweetbreads on all sides in the butter over medium-high heat. Add the mirepoix of vegetables.

Cover the pan and place in a 210 C (400 F) oven for about

5 minutes to cook the vegetables. Stir the vegetables after a couple of minutes so that they cook evenly.

When the vegetables are soft, pour off the cooking fat and deglaze with 1 dl (1/2 cup) of sherry vinegar. Cover and return the pot to the oven until the liquid is reduced by half.

Add 1/4 L (1 cup) of demi-glace (reduced veal stock), season with salt and pepper to taste, cover and finish the braising process in the oven.

Cooking time will vary, depending on the size of the sweetbreads-about 8-10 minutes.

It is important not to overcook the sweetbreads as they will become dry and tough. The tender, "melt in your mouth" quality of the sweetbreads will make these hors d'œuvres delicious.

When braising is complete, remove the sweetbreads to a plate and set aside. Reserve the pot with the braising juices to make the sauce.

Making the Sherry Vinegar Sauce

Pass the braising juice through a fine-meshed conical sieve. Reduce these juices by half and whisk in enough cooked roux to thicken the sauce slightly. Add 2 dl (3/4 cup) heavy cream and simmer briefly, skimming the foam that rises to the surface.

Season to taste. Pass the sauce through a strainer and whisk in a little butter.

Assembly

Fill the bottom of the croustades with a spoonful of mushroom duxelles. Slice the braised sweetbreads in pieces about the size of the croustade and place one piece on top of the duxelles. Cover the piece of sweetbreads with a spoonful of sauce, taking care not to drip sauce on the sides of the pastry shell.

Presentation

Warm the hors d'œuvres in a 180 C (350 F) oven for a few minutes. Arrange on a platter and serve immediately.

Chapter 6
Centerpieces for Buffets

〜〜〜〜〜〜〜〜〜

Enhance Your Receptions

These centerpieces add a glamorous and original note to a buffet.

For small receptions, one of these centerpieces can be chosen to serve as the main attraction along with a selection of hot and cold hors d'œuvres.

For grand occasions with many guests, several centerpieces can be used for a dramatic effect as well as providing a large number of refreshments in an attractive "package".

These centerpieces become

part of the decoration of the buffet, furnishing dimension and color like the floral arrangements. The artistic execution of these displays is therefore very important.

Sandwiches and filled rolls in a variety of shapes and flavors can enter into the making of the "Drakkar" and "Surprise Breads".

For the centerpieces using a base with items attached by toothpicks, any number of small hors-d'œuvres can be served (colorful crudités and filled crêpes are pictured here). The cold brochettes, for example, can be made small enough to serve as appetizers and would be lovely presented attached to an appropriate base.

"Pains Surprises" (Surprise Breads)

The name surprise breads appropriately describes these decorative containers that hold a hidden supply of sandwiches.

The inside of the bread is carefully carved out, then sliced thinly. The slices are spread with a variety of fillings, cut into small sandwiches, then placed back inside, and the top of the bread is replaced to form the lid and keep the sandwiches fresh.

Surprise breads can be made with any close-textured bread including:
"Pain de mie" (milk-enriched white bread)
Brioche (egg and butter enriched bread)

Rye or whole wheat bread with:

- herbs
- olives
- walnuts
- raisins

The flavored breads should marry well with the flavor of the fillings.

The bread containers can be baked in different forms and in various sizes to suit the occasion.

They are usually baked in a mold, but in some cases can be formed by hand.

The top can be left plain (in this case, often a bow is attached), or a decoration can be made from dough and baked on the top.

Cutting Out Surprise Breads

Whatever bread you choose, it should be made 24-48 hours in advance, which makes it easier to carve out and slice.

They can be made in sizeable batches and frozen until ready to use.

To remove the inside in one neat piece, the method is the same for any of the different breads pictured.

Use a knife that has a stiff blade, is well-sharpened and easy to handle, which ensures clean, neat cuts.

To carve out the inside of the

bread, cut a border around the top about 1.5 cm (1/2 in) wide to mark the outside "walls" of the container.

Whichever shape of bread you are working with, simply follow the form of the crust and leave the bor-

der as described. Once you have cut around the top to mark the border, follow this cut around the edge, and with the knife straight up and down, cut down to the bottom without cutting through the base.

To remove the inside of a rectangular loaf in a neat piece, make an

incision on one side of the container about 1.5 cm (1/2 in) from the bottom. Leave the crust intact at either end. For round loaves, insert the blade of the knife at the base, then pivot it one way, turn the blade around and pivot in the other direction to cut the base of the bread.

Turn the loaf upside down and let the inside of the bread slip out.

Cutting the Slices

For neat, even slices, use a long serrated knife or an electric slicer. For the denser breads that have a tendency to stick to the knife (rye, for instance), apply a little oil to the knife before each slice.

To avoid waste, measure out the number of slices so that they are the same thickness and that there are an even number to accommodate the two slices needed to form the sandwiches.

Like the mini-sandwiches described in Chapter 2, before the sandwiches are filled, the slices are often coated with the following ingredients to protect the bread and add flavor:

- Salted or flavored butters
- Mayonnaise seasoned with herbs or spices
- Mousses or creams that are applied directly to the bread

A rectangular board is used, as shown, to press gently on the sandwiches to stick the layers together.

To get neat sandwiches that are all the same size, the filled slices are stacked on top of each other, then the edges are trimmed and the slices are cut into small sandwiches whatever size suits the occasion.

Surprise Bread with Walnuts and Raisins

This surprise bread is simple to make and is always popular. It can be made two ways:

- The raisins can be baked directly into the bread, then the bread is coated with ground walnuts mixed with butter.
- Raisins that have been softened by blanching can be chopped and mixed with ground walnuts. This mixture is then applied evenly between two slices of plain bread that has been coated with salted butter.

Currants or golden raisins give the best result for this preparation.

Surprise Bread with Olives, Crab and Watercress

This delicious combination is a little out of the ordinary. The olive bread goes very well with raw vegetables and salads, in this case watercress.

Coat the slices with mayonnaise. Remove the leaves of watercress from the stem and spread them evenly over the coated slice of bread. Add a thin layer of flaked crab meat, then cover with a second slice of coated olive bread. Stack the filled slices, then trim the edges and cut into sandwiches.

Place the sandwiches neatly back into the bread case and replace the lid to keep them fresh.

Refrigerate until ready to serve.

Surprise Bread with Ham and Swiss Cheese

NOTE: "Pain de mie" (milk-enriched white bread) is the bread most frequently used for surprise breads.

Although it has slightly less "character" than other more full-flavored breads, it will readily complement any type of filling, making it easy to accommodate last-minute requests.

The caterer must guide the client in his selection of fillings to avoid inappropriate combinations. To keep the work manageable, three different fillings per surprise bread is the maximum.

Ham and swiss cheese are good fillings that are natural partners. Be sure always to use a good quality boiled or baked ham, and choose one of the many delicious swiss-type cheeses available, such as Gruyère, Emmenthal, Fribourg, Appenzeller or Comté.

Spread a thin coat of salted butter on the sliced white bread. When replacing the sandwiches in the hollowed out loaf, arrange the slices so there are alternating layers of ham and cheese.

Surprise Bread

Surprise Bread
with Cumin, Roquefort and Walnuts

This cumin bread can be baked in different shapes, including small loaves designed to serve just a few people.

Cream the roquefort, then blend in softened butter in the ratio of 4 parts cheese to 1 part butter. Spread

the slices of bread with a thin coat of this mixture. Sprinkle with chopped walnuts, lay the slices on top of each other and press gently to seal.

Slice the bread into small sandwiches and arrange in the hollow crust.

The bread can be sliced either horizontally or vertically, depending on the shape and size of the loaf. Each method will yield a slightly different presentation.

with Chicken and Herbs

Spread slices of white bread with a thin coat of mayonnaise. Use chicken that has been poached in chicken stock and thoroughly cooled. Remove the skin and cut the meat from the bones, then cut or pull the chicken into small pieces. Arrange the chicken on the prepared slices, then sprinkle with an assortment of chopped fresh herbs according to your taste (chervil, tarragon, chives). Cover with a second prepared slice of bread and press gently to seal.

Round Surprise Breads

These round loaves for surprise breads are usually made with rye bread-either light, medium or dark.

The dough is shaped and baked in a round mold. Use a deep springform pan or a bottomless ring mold that is set directly on a round baking sheet. The size of the mold will vary with the amount of dough used.

The loaves can be decorated in a festive manner using a yeastless bread dough ("pâte morte", or "dead dough"), from which leaves, flowers, bows and other shapes are fashioned.

After kneading the dough, nuts, raisins and other dried fruits may be worked in.

Many combinations of fillings may be used. After adding the filling, cut the bread into triangular sandwiches and arrange them in the hollow loaf in a slightly overlapping pattern. This makes the surprise bread look very full and appetizing, and it makes the sandwiches easy to remove.

Brioches "Mousseline"

Brioche "mousseline" (the name given to light-textured tall cylindrical loaves) is another type of bread that lends itself to surprise breads.

It is quite difficult to hollow out a regular size brioche mousseline, so the method described here involves simply slicing the whole loaf and keeping the bottom and top slices ungarnished to serve as the base and lid for the stack of sandwiches.

Usually, the slices of brioche mousseline are spread with a thin coat of flavored butter (crab, salmon, foie gras).

Another good filling would be mayonnaise mixed with flaked crab and chopped chervil.

Brioches "Mousseline"

Whatever the filling used, its texture should be as soft as the texture of the bread for easy spreading.

After spreading a slice with the filling and covering with a second slice, cut the sandwiches in quarters.

Stack them carefully on the ungarnished base slice, rotating each layer by about a quarter turn to give the stack stability.

Surprise Breads with Preserved Meats

For preserved meat surprise breads, a round loaf of pain de mie or whole wheat bread is a good choice.

Spread the slices with a thin coat of salted butter.

Use just one or a combination of the following fillings.

- Country ham

- Boiled ham

- Dried or smoked ham (such as Parma)

- Dry sausage

- Salami

- Garlic sausage (plain or smoked)

- Andouilles

- Mortadella

General Notes on Shaping and Stacking the Sandwiches

The slicing and arrangement of the sandwiches will differ depending on the shape of the loaf used for the surprise bread and the choice of filling.

When using filling such as the preserved meats shown here, the appearance of the sandwiches can be improved by trimming the edges with a sharp serrated knife and a round guide, such as the removable bottom of a tart pan.

The sandwiches can be arranged in the hollow loaf in many ways, including the overlapping pattern

mentioned on p. 166 and shown below or in a straight tight-fitting stack, also pictured on this page.

To make this easier, do not separate the sandwiches after cutting them, but rather place one whole stack at a time in the loaf container.

Surprise breads are always very popular at all kinds of functions, ranging from a small reception to a lunch or even a large buffet. Choose an interesting combination of fillings so there will be something to suit everyone's taste. The lids can be decorated with "pâte morte", as described on p. 166, or if the lid is left plain, a fabric or paper ribbon in colors matching the decor of the reception can be attached.

Surprise Breads with Crudités

Fresh raw vegetables (crudités) are delicious on olive bread, but crudité surprise breads made with white bread are also a good choice and are less expensive to produce.

For these crudité sandwiches, spread the slices of bread with a thin coat of plain or flavored mayonnaise. The vegetables can be sliced very thinly or even grated, but in any case, season them well so the sandwiches are not bland.

These sandwiches are very refreshing and light. As with all the surprise breads described in this chapter, the manner in which these sandwiches are sliced depends on the shape of the loaf.

Always cut the sandwiches so they are even.

For the large oval loaf pictured below, more or less rectangular-shaped sandwiches are cut from the middle, with triangular ones cut from the two rounded ends. The sandwiches are stacked straight in, rather than overlapped as in many of the round surprise bread presentations.

Surprise Breads with Fish

As with the preserved meats and crudité sandwiches, these sandwiches can be filled with one or a combination of fillings, in this case, fish-based, such as:

Fish eggs: salmon, lumpfish

Smoked fish: trout, salmon, eel

Fish mousse: trout, salmon

Rye bread or white bread are the best choices for the base. Spread the sliced bread with a thin coat of salted butter and add the desired filling or fillings to produce a flavorful and interesting assortment.

Louis XIV Brioche

Brioche dough can be made into loaves of many forms.

For this spectacular Louis XIV brioche, hollow out a large traditionally-shaped brioche ("brioche à tête"), cut the center into slices, and spread them with the selected filling.

As with the brioche mousseline, make sure the filling has a soft and spreadable enough texture for the delicate brioche, for example a flavored butter or a mousse.

Cut the slices into triangular sandwiches one layer at a time, as each layer will have a different diameter and therefore will yield a different number of sandwiches.

A Variety of Surprise Breads

Different Shapes and Fillings

The Canapé "Hedgehog"

A Spectacular Display !

This whimsical and appealing "hedgehog" of skewered canapés is the result of two techniques.

A cube of white bread is wrapped with a slice of flavorful ingredients such as cured ham (Parma, for example) or smoked salmon.

The cubes are skewered with toothpicks, which are inserted into a base made from a round styrofoam form or a large round melon. The centerpiece may be given extra dimension by carving the base into a decorative shape.

Shaping the Bread Cubes

Trim the ends off the bread with a stiff serrated knife. With the aid of metal "candy rulers" (available in professional kitchenware shops), or similarly shaped rods, guide the knife to obtain even, uniform slices. The "ruler" is then used to cut the slices into strips the size of the ruler (about 1.5 cm (1/2 in)). Discard the crusts.

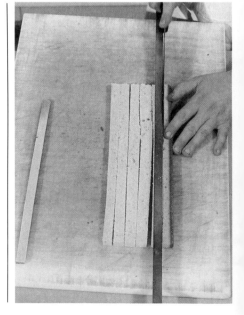

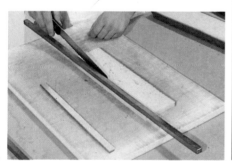

Cut bands of parchment paper that are the same length as the bread strips and 1 1/2 times as wide as the circumference of the strips.

Lay the strips on a clean sheet pan and brush on a very thin coat of oil. Cut the Parma ham on the electric slicer and the smoked salmon by hand into very fine slices and arrange them neatly in a single layer on the oiled parchment paper (as shown).

Put the pans in the freezer for a few minutes to set so that the ingredients will be easier to coat with butter.

Using a pastry brush, spread a thin layer of creamed butter on the chilled bands of ham and salmon.

The Canapé "Hedgehog" (continued)

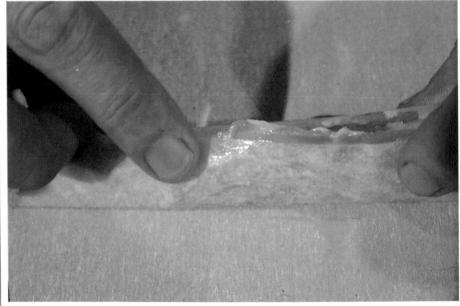

Let the bands return to room temperature, then lay a bread strip on one long edge and roll up so the bread is neatly and completely covered and the ham or salmon overlaps by a quarter width to seal. (Take care not to roll the edge of the parchment paper inside, as it will be difficult to remove when the strips are frozen.)

The Canapé "Hedgehog" (continued)

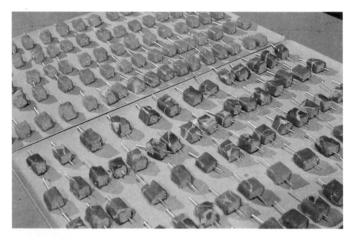

Press gently on all four sides of the canapé strips with a palette knife to make sure that the ham or salmon is firmly adhered to the bread. Freeze the canapé strips.

To finish, carefully peel the parchment paper from the frozen strips and slice into even pieces about 2 cm (3/4 in) long.

Push a toothpick through the cut side of a cube as shown until the point extends enough on the other side so the cube can be firmly inserted in the styrofoam or melon base.

Arrange the pierced cubes evenly over the base, starting at the top, placing them in neat rows. For decoration, a few frilled toothpicks may be incorporated in the design.

A time-saving and effective technique is to prepare canapé strips well in advance and keep them frozen in tightly sealed boxes until needed.

If the "hedgehog" is made a few hours before presentation, keep it moist by covering it with a damp cloth, moistened parchment paper or aluminum foil and refrigerate.

181

Stuffed Crêpe "Hedgehog"

This "hedgehog" is made of small rolls created by rolling flavorful fillings in a crêpe and slicing the roll into pieces.

Use a classic recipe for crêpes, eliminating any sugar in the recipe and adding a few finely chopped herbs (chervil, tarragon, chives) to make them more flavorful.

The crêpes can be cooked in a classic round pan or the batter can be poured in a thin layer onto a buttered sheet pan and baked.

The rectangular shape of the latter is easy to fill and roll and does not need to be trimmed.

Round crêpes need to be "squared off" before filling so that filling is not wasted.

In either case, do not overcook the crêpes, as they will dry out and be difficult to roll.

The cooked crêpes are set aside to cool completely before filling.

Filling and Rolling the Crêpes

The crêpes can be filled with a variety of ingredients, including the following:

a) Fish and seafood: lumpfish eggs, salmon eggs, salmon butter, anchovy butter, crab butter, other seafood butters (sardine, trout, tuna, eel), crab with mayonnaise, smoked salmon

b) Prepared meats

c) Cheeses

Some fillings are a single ingredient (Parma ham, smoked salmon, salami, for example). For these, the crêpes are coated with a thin layer of butter or mayonnaise first.

The ingredient is laid out on top, then a little more butter or mayonnaise is brushed or spread on top so when the crêpe is rolled, it will stick.

For mixtures, ingredients need to be chopped or flaked finely so that they are spread easily on the crêpe (crab with mayonnaise, for example).

These mixtures, which include flavored butters, cheeses and foie gras, are spread directly on the crêpes.

In all cases, the filling should be applied evenly and amply enough to create a tasty hors-d'œuvre without making the rolled crêpe too thick to slice properly.

Stuffed Crêpe "Hedgehog" (continued)

Assembly

Once filled, roll the crêpes tightly without tearing them. Press gently on the edge to stick it to the filling so the crêpe does not unroll.

Place the rolled crêpes in the refrigerator for at least an hour to set the ingredients and make slicing easier.

The crêpes can be prepared to this point the day before, covered in plastic wrap and stored in the refrigerator.

The chilled rolled crêpes are cut into small pieces about 1 cm (3/8 in) long. This recommended size is large enough to hold well on the toothpick and yet is still small enough to be "bite size".

Push a toothpick through each spiral as pictured on the opposite page with the edge of the crêpe at the top of the toothpick to keep it from unrolling.

A Variety of Bases

These hors-d'œuvres can be attached to a variety of different bases to suit the occasion.

Bases made of cork or styrofoam can be shaped (carved) to coordinate with the flavor of the crêpes.

For example, crêpes filled with seafood can be attached to a base in the form of a fish (as shown in this chapter) or shell.

Presentation

These bases are usually covered with aluminum foil, and in the case of the fish, can be further embellished with thin overlapping slices of cucumber to simulate scales. This glamorous presentation is then glazed with aspic before attaching the toothpicks.

Pumpkins or small watermelons can also be used as bases.

The flavors can be mixed on one base, which makes a very colorful presentation.

The "hedgehog" can be further decorated with colorful crudités on toothpicks, for example, pickled vegetables, chanterelles, baby vegetables, spring onions, baby ears of corn, sweet peppers, cherry tomatoes.

This centerpiece can be made in advance and kept fresh by covering with a damp hand towel or moistened parchment paper and wrapped in foil and kept in the refrigerator.

These original hors-d'œuvres are a welcome change of pace on the buffet table.

Stuffed Crêpe "Hedgehog" (continued)

The "Drakkar"

Unlike the other centerpieces in this chapter, the "Drakkar" (or Viking ship) is not easily adaptable to different sizes. It is made to accommodate a rectangular loaf of "pain de mie" (enriched white bread), which serves as the base. The loaf of bread is trimmed at both ends, so that a cardboard form in the shape of an oval boat will slide down snugly around it. The cardboard "hull" of the drakkar is made

Shaping the Cardboard Ship

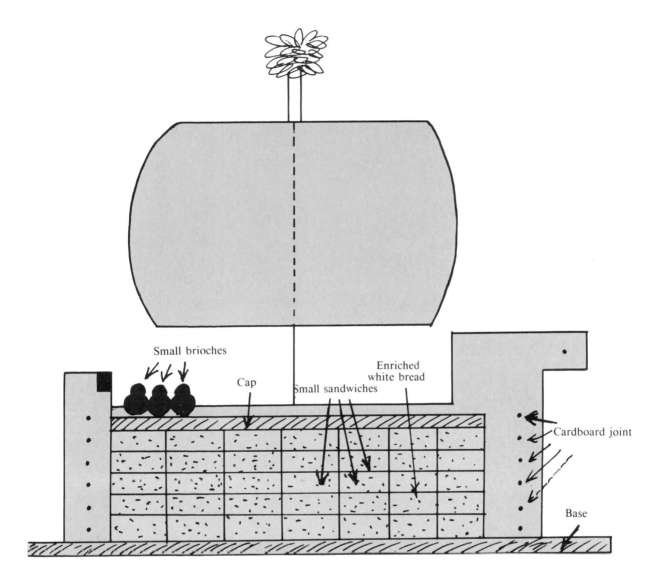

Small brioches

Cap

Small sandwiches

Enriched
white bread

Cardboard joint

Base

Cross section of the loaf of bread, from above

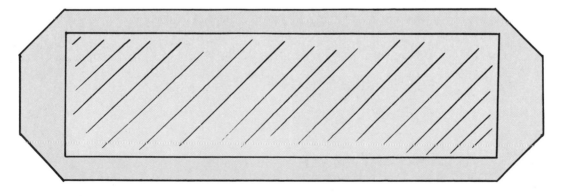

from metallic covered cardboard that is cut to fit the loaf of bread.

Therefore, depending on the volume of business, a caterer may have "Drakkars" available in two or three sizes.

The assembly of the drakkar is a combination of three preparations that have been presented in this volume:

a) surprise breads

b) small filled brioches

c) two types of decorated canapés

The "Drakkar" (continued)

The loaf of bread is trimmed at both ends as shown, then the inside is carved out (see p. 162), leaving a case of bread to hold the sandwiches and serve as the hull of the ship.

The inside of the bread is sliced and filled, cut into sandwiches and placed back into the crust case.

The hull made of metallic colored cardboard is fitted around the bread, and the ship is placed on a sturdy rectangle of cardboard covered with aluminum foil, or directly on a platter.

Mini brioches (with the traditional top knot or "head") are made in tartelette molds to repre-

sent the "Vikings" in the boat. The baked brioches are hollowed out and filled with a mousse (crab, foie gras or cheese).

The brioches with "heads" placed on top of the filling are then arranged in rows on top of the loaf of bread.

To finish the presentation, round canapés are made to represent the Viking shields and triangular canapés are made to represent the oars of the boat.

To apply these decorations, push a toothpick into the canapés and place the round ones along the top edge of the boat (at an angle, as shown), and set the triangular ones along the base, with the toothpicks pointing up.

A cardbord "sail" on a large wooden skewer is placed in the center of the boat.

The "Drakkar" (continued)

To personalize this centerpiece for a special occasion, the name of a guest of honor, a greeting or a message can be written on the sail--a gesture that always pleases the customers.

Since the preparation of the drakkar is relatively long due to the many elements that go into its completion, it is a more expensive item.

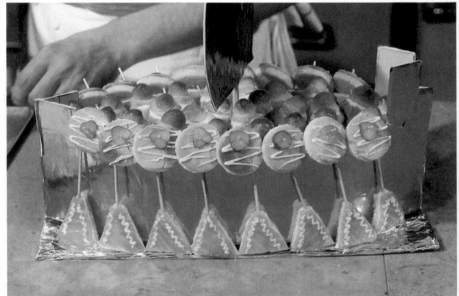

It is ideal for large buffets because it holds a large number of hors-d'œuvres and adds a dramatic note to the arrangement of the table.

Your customers will enjoy this original and decorative centerpiece.

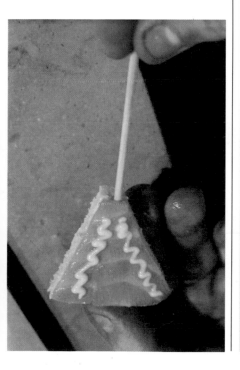

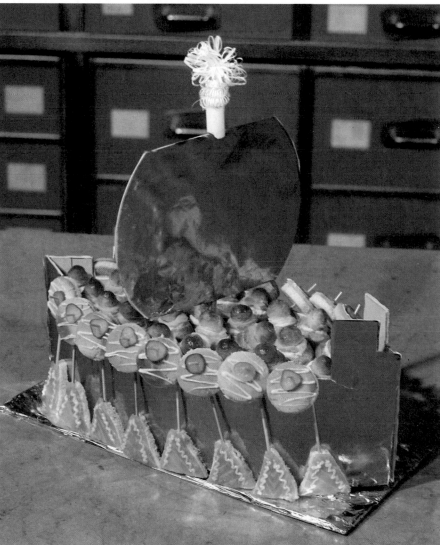

Bouquet of Crudités

A Fresh and Colorful Display !

What better way to start a buffet than with refreshing crudités dipped in a tasty sauce?

This festive bouquet of vegetables is a colorful decoration on the buffet table.

It can be made in any size to accommodate the number of guests.

The caterer can vary the base according to the occasion. For the bouquet presented here, a tray made of cork is used to hold the large vegetables into which the crudités on toothpicks are placed. The rustic, natural look of the cork tray makes an appropriate base. Wicker baskets would also be appropriate.

The large vegetables and fruits that serve as a support for the crudités can vary as well. For larger arrangements, a small watermelon or pumpkin can be used, as shown in the "Stuffed Crêpe Hedgehog". The melon is then surrounded with other fruits and vegetables to add dimension and color.

As we see in the photographs, a wide assortment of fruits and vegetables can be used for the support. For example: green and red cabbage, grapefruit, artichokes, cucumbers, red and green peppers, large tomatoes, and melons and squash in all sizes.

Lovely branches of greenery can be placed among the fresh produce to make the bouquet complete.

The arrangement of the support is very important to the balance and colorful presentation of the crudités.

The next step is to prepare the bite size crudités which are put on toothpicks and attached to the fruit and vegetable base.

All of the vegetables are raw, except the beets and small ears of corn, which are sold already cooked.

The vegetables are washed thoroughly. The small ones, like the radishes, are trimmed and presented whole. Larger vegetables are peeled and either cut into cubes or "turned" into neat oval shapes. It is important that all the crudités are about the same size. Use a radish or cherry tomato as a guide to determine the size of the other vegetables that are cut into pieces.

It is also important that the prepared vegetables be as uniform as possible for an attractive display.

Those vegetables that have a tendancy to darken should be sprinkled with a little lemon juice to maintain their color.

Choose fruits and vegetables that are in season, therefore changing your selection to suit what is best at the market.

On the next page, vegetables are shown trimmed and ready to be skewered and secured to the support.

Turned: Carrots, cucumbers.

Cut in small pieces: melons, celery, red peppers, green peppers, cauliflower, mushrooms, corn.

Left whole: radishes, pearl onions, cherry tomatoes.

The 14 Crudités (details)

Assembly of the Bouquet of Crudités

When all the vegetables are prepared, push a toothpick through each one so that the point extends about 2 cm (3/4 in).

Attach the crudités to the arranged vegetable and fruit support, taking care to intersperse the colors and shapes to create a pretty bouquet.

This centerpiece is not difficult or expensive to make, however the preparation time is quite long because of the number of ingredients used.

The "Bouquet of Crudités" can be assembled several hours in advance and covered with a damp hand towel and refrigerated until ready to serve.

Sauces made with mayonnaise and flavored with herbs and spices are usually serve alongside the crudités.

Chapter 7 – Cold Brochettes

~~~~~~~~~~~~~~~~~~~

In this chapter, we present six different types of cold brochettes using chicken, beef, lamb, ham, fish and shellfish as the main ingredients. They also feature garnishes of vegetables and fruits that complement the main ingredient. After they are assembled, they are glazed with a lightly jellied sauce and/or aspic which makes them more attractive, enhances their flavor and keeps them fresh.

The chef can use his creativity when making cold brochettes. The well balanced colors and subtle flavor combinations are particularly pleasing to customers. Cold brochettes are really quite unlike their grilled cousins, being more refined and sophisticated.

Different Presentations for Different Uses

These brochettes can be made in a variety of sizes depending on how they will be served. They can be arranged in many different ways to create magnificent plates, platters and centerpieces.

Buffets and Receptions

Often cold brochettes are presented on a base of styrofoam or cork which puts them in a place of prominence and also serves as a decoration on the buffet. They can also be arranged on platters. They are always a very popular item among the cold hors d'œuvres.

Cold First Courses and Snacks

They are light and refreshing and easy to handle. Accompanied by a salad and made in different sizes, cold brochettes can be a versatile part of a menu.

Retail

In a specialty food shop, cold brochettes can be arranged on plates or platters to be sold individually or placed in disposible containers to be sold by the dozen.

General Guidelines for the Preparation of Cold Brochettes

Ingredients

It is very important to use only top quality, choice ingredients. When purchasing the main ingredients, the following are recommended:

Chicken: use only the breast meat

Beef: choose the filet or strip

Lamb: use the leg of lamb

Ham: purchase a top quality boiled or baked ham

Fish: work with monkfish and dover sole

Shellfish: use medium shrimp, mussels and bay scallops

Choose fruits and vegetables that are vibrant and unblemished. The colors and flavors should complement and enhance the main ingredients.

The jellied sauces and/or aspic used to glaze these brochettes should be light yet well seasoned. The flavor of the sauce is the personal note of the chef that distinguishes these brochettes. These specially prepared sauces not only enhance the flavor, but also make the brochettes shine, making for a dazzling presentation. In addition, it keeps them moist and fresh until they are ready to serve.

Our Selection

Chicken Brochettes Glazed with Herb Chaud-froid

Cubed chicken, mushrooms, pearl onions, carrots, herb chaud-froid

Ham and Pineapple Brochettes

Cubed ham, pineapple, cherries, sweet and sour pineapple sauce

Curried Lamb Brochettes

Cubed leg of lamb, apples, bananas, pineapple, curry sauce

Fish and Vegetable Brochettes

Cubed monkfish and sole, scallop coral, zucchinis, carrots, cucumbers, saffron aspic

Beef Stroganoff Brochettes

Cubed beef filet, green peppers, pearl onions, cherry tomatoes, stroganoff sauce

Shellfish and Tropical Fruit Brochettes

Mussels, bay scallops, shrimp, limes, mangoes, kiwis, anise aspic

Procedure

Since you will be working with many components, it is important that you work very methodically. Before starting, verify that all of the ingredients are on hand, including those needed to make the sauce. Gather all of the equipment necessary to prepare and assemble the brochettes.

Preparing the Main Ingredients and Garnishes

Meats: Carefully trim all fat and nerves.
Fish: Neatly skin and remove all bones.
Shellfish: Clean thoroughly, carefully remove from shells.

Vegetables and fruits: Peel carefully and neatly and wash thoroughly. Use lemon juice to rub or sprinkle on garnishes that have a tendency to oxidize and darken (apples, bananas, and mushrooms).

Cutting and Shaping

To obtain uniform brochettes, it is important to realize that almost all of the ingredients are cooked and therefore their appearance will change. While cutting and shaping the ingredients, take this into consideration so that all of the components to be assembled are about the same size.

Cooking the Ingredients

Several methods of cooking are used depending on the ingredient:
Pan fry or sauté: Chicken, beef, lamb, green peppers
Poach: Fish and scallops in court bouillon or fish stock; chicken in chicken stock; pineapple in light syrup; cherries in wine
Steam "à la marinière": Mussels
Blanch: Cucumbers, zucchini, carrots
Glaze: Onions, carrots

Assembling the Brochettes

Alternate pieces of the main ingredient and the garnishes to obtain colorful brochettes. (Assemble each type of brochette in the same order for a uniform presentation.)

Preparation of Cold Brochettes

Procedure for Cold Brochettes

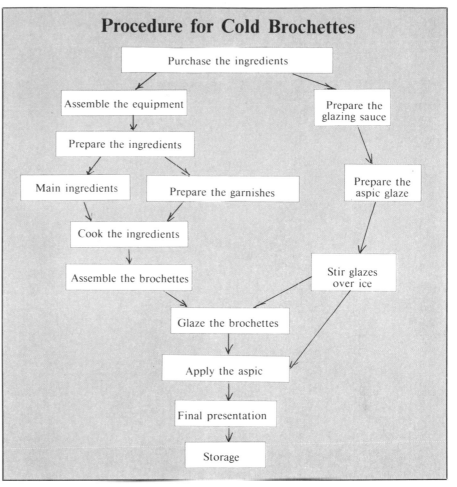

Carefully skewer each ingredient so it holds solidly in place. Choose a sturdy ingredient to place at either end to insure easy handling.

Glazing the Brochettes

To properly set the jellied sauce and aspic, the brochettes must be thoroughly chilled before glazing.

Applying two layers of sauce improves the appearance and taste of the brochettes.

Adding a final coat of clear aspic makes them shine and protects them.

Use a soft brush to apply the aspic, so you don't damage the glaze.

Profitability

It is desirable to make at least 20 of each type at a time.

When a large order is placed, suggest a varied assortment that contains a balance of meat or chicken, fish or shellfish, fruit and vegetables.

Take into consideration that customers enjoy trying new and creative taste combinations.

Chicken Brochettes Glazed with Herb Chaud-froid

Introduction

These brochettes are certainly the most classic of the six types presented in this chapter.

They are glazed with a light mayonnaise based sauce flavored with an assortment of fresh herbs.

The vegetable garnishes (carrots, pearl onions, mushrooms) marry well with the subtle flavor and golden color of the chicken.

These delicate brochettes are always very popular at receptions.

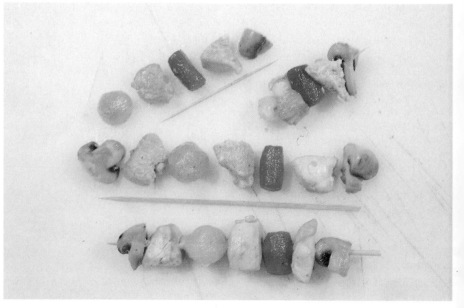

Equipment

Cutting board, thin-bladed knife, vegetable peeler, paring knife, chef's knife, wooden skewers, sauté pan with cover, saucepan, mixing bowls, conical strainer, whisk, sheet pan for draining, cooling rack, tablespoon, skimmer, hand towels, parchment paper, soft-bristled pastry brush

Ingredients

The Main Ingredient

You may choose to purchase the whole chicken, using the breast meat for these brochettes and using the rest in another dish. In this case you will have the carcass which can serve to make the aspic.

Turkey breast may also be used which is usually less expensive but not as flavorful.

The cubes of chicken (or turkey) can be poached or sautéed requiring the following ingredients:

For poaching: chicken stock; a finely diced mixture of carrots, celery, onions, leeks, garlic and shallots (mirepoix) tied in cheesecloth, bouquet garni, salt and peppercorns.

For sautéing: clarified butter, salt and pepper.

The Garnish

Glazed carrots: water, butter, sugar, salt, pepper.

Glazed onions: water, butter, sugar, salt pepper. Cooked mushrooms: lemon juice, water, butter, salt, pepper.

Procedure

Preparing the Main Ingredient

Spread the breasts out on the cutting board and carefully remove the skin and fat without damaging the meat.

With a well sharpened thin bladed knife, trim all tendons. Trimming the chicken should be done with great care so that you can cut neat cubes of meat which will insure attractive brochettes that are easy to assemble.

Once trimmed, cut the meat in cubes. The size will depend on how the brochettes will be served. It is very important to remember that the chicken or turkey, no longer supported by the bone, will shrink during cooking (the shrinkage will be about 1/3 of original size).

Cooking the Main Ingredient

If you are going to sauté the chicken, melt a little butter in a sauté pan large enough to fit all of the chicken in a single layer. Salt and pepper the chicken.

When the butter is hot but not brown, add the chicken pieces and turn them with a wooden spatula so they cook evenly.

When the meat is lightly browned, cooked thoroughly and still moist, remove to a shallow pan, as shown, to drain. Set aside.

If you choose to poach the cubes of chicken, spread them on the bottom of the pan and cover with chicken stock. Add the finely chopped vegetables wrapped in cheesecloth and the bouquet garni. (These vegetables augment the flavor, and bundled in cheesecloth are easy to remove after cooking.)

It is very important to start the poaching in cold stock and slowly bring the stock to a simmer. Poach gently for about 5-6 minutes depending on the size of the cubes. Do not overcook as the chicken will shrink and dry out.

As soon as the chicken is cooked, remove the pan from the heat and let the chicken cool in the stock. This keeps the meat moist and allows the meat to absorb all the flavor from the stock and vegetables.

When cool, drain and reserve until you are ready to assemble the brochettes.

Preparing the Garnish

Choose the Ingredients Carefully

The freshness and size of the vegetables and fruits are very important so that they can be trimmed and shaped rapidly into even pieces with minimum waste. This will keep food costs down.

The Mushrooms

Choose large, white, firm mushrooms. Remove sand or dirt from stems by trimming the stems to a point with a paring knife.

Wash the mushrooms in a large basin of cold water, changing the water several times until no sand or dirt is left in the bottom. The mushrooms should not soak in the water as they will darken and become soggy.

Cut the mushrooms in 1/2 (or in quarters, depending on the size of the mushrooms and the size of the brochettes to be made) and sprinkle the pieces with lemon juice.

Cooking the Mushrooms

Cook the mushrooms in a small amount of water with butter, salt and pepper.

Bring this cooking liquid to a boil then add the mushrooms and cover tightly. Return the pot to high heat and bring the water back to a boil as quickly as possible. (Depending on the size of the pieces, count on about 5-10 minutes to cook them.) Remove them to a stainless steel receptacle so they will not oxidize and set aside to cool. (The liquid rendered by the mushrooms can be reserved for another use.)

The Glazed Onions

Choose small bite size onions.

In spring, white or "spring" onions are a good choice. They are usually sold in bunches with the green sprouts attached. Trim the white root of the onion and use the green portion in stock.

Pearl onions are almost always available. These are sold by the pound and are covered with a white papery skin.

Cooking the Onions

In the bottom of a saucepan, spread the onions in a single layer so they will cook quickly and glaze evenly.

Add water to cover by about 2/3 (a little less water is required for spring onions). Season with a pinch of salt and a little freshly ground pepper. Add approximately 8 teaspoons of sugar per cup of water.

Cut a circle of parchment paper the size of the saucepan and place it directly on top of the onions.

Usually the onions are cooked when the liquid has evaporated, leaving a little butter in the bottom. The sugar will have cooked to a light caramel, forming a syrup with the butter that lightly coats each onion.

Remove the onions to a plate to cool.

The Glazed Carrots

There are two criteria to consider when choosing the carrots: size and texture. It is recommended to choose medium sized carrots that will be of an even color throughout and not fibrous in the middle.

Cut the carrots in sections about an inch long. Divide thicker pieces in half so that they are all about the same size.

Shape or "turn" the carrots with a paring knife to obtain pieces about the size and shape of a large clove of garlic. Trimming vegetables in this way requires skill and attention to produce even shapes that will cook and glaze evenly.

Cooking the Carrots

Follow the same procedure described for the glazed onions. A little more water is needed as the carrots take longer to cook.

When they are cooked through and glazed, remove immediately to a plate to cool completely.

Preparing the Herb Chaud-froid

This chaud-froid is made with mayonnaise and chicken aspic. The proportions are 1/3 mayonnaise to 2/3 aspic. To combine these two ingredients, melt the aspic over low heat. When liquid but still cool, stir into the mayonnaise. This should be done just before you are ready to glaze the brochettes.

The sauce is embellished with an addition of "fines herbes" (usually a combination of chervil (or parsley), chives and tarragon). Chop the chervil and tarragon finely. The chives should be carefully chopped separately, starting from one end for a neater result. Use a well sharpened chef's knife to chop the herbs. Blend the prepared herbs into the chaud-froid.

Assembling the Brochettes

Gather together all of the prepared ingredients and the wooden skewers.

To make attractive brochettes, remember to alternate the ingredients, playing with varied colors of the chicken and garnishes.

Make sure that the ingredients are secure on the skewers. To hold them in place, choose a firm ingredient at either end. Once assembled, chill until ready to glaze.

Glazing the Brochettes

The brochettes must be thoroughly chilled before you begin to glaze.

To thicken the chaud-froid so that it will coat properly, stir the prepared sauce over crushed ice until it starts to set slightly but is still liquid, stirring constantly with a whisk or wooden spoon to avoid lumps.

When the sauce is ready, apply the first layer by holding each brochette over the bowl of sauce as shown, and brushing on the sauce to coat evenly.

Place the glazed brochettes on a rack placed on a clean baking sheet to drain.

Chill the brochettes to set the first layer of sauce.

Bring the sauce back to the proper consistency, apply a second layer of sauce and return to the refrigerator.

This refreshing chaud-froid with its tasty addition of herbs rounds out the delicious flavor of these brochettes and is the personal note of the chef.

Final Aspic Glaze

Adding a final coat of aspic made from chicken stock protects and conserves the brochettes and makes them shine.

This aspic can be flavored with wine, port, or sherry.

Final Presentation

Arrange on plates, platters or secure them to a base.

Storage

These brochettes are very perishable. To maintain freshness, taste and a lovely appearance, they should be kept chilled until you are ready to serve them.

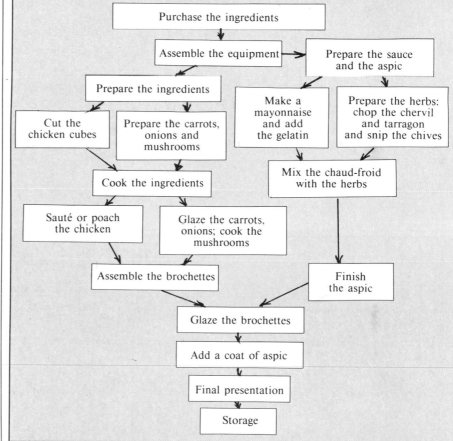

Chicken and Herb Brochettes

Purchase the ingredients → Assemble the equipment → Prepare the sauce and the aspic

Assemble the equipment → Prepare the ingredients

Prepare the sauce and the aspic → Make a mayonnaise and add the gelatin

Prepare the sauce and the aspic → Prepare the herbs: chop the chervil and tarragon and snip the chives

Prepare the ingredients → Cut the chicken cubes

Prepare the ingredients → Prepare the carrots, onions and mushrooms

Cut the chicken cubes → Cook the ingredients

Prepare the carrots, onions and mushrooms → Cook the ingredients

Make a mayonnaise and add the gelatin → Mix the chaud-froid with the herbs

Prepare the herbs → Mix the chaud-froid with the herbs

Cook the ingredients → Sauté or poach the chicken

Cook the ingredients → Glaze the carrots, onions; cook the mushrooms

Sauté or poach the chicken → Assemble the brochettes

Mix the chaud-froid with the herbs → Finish the aspic

Assemble the brochettes → Glaze the brochettes

Finish the aspic → Glaze the brochettes

Glaze the brochettes → Add a coat of aspic → Final presentation → Storage

Beef Strogonoff Brochettes

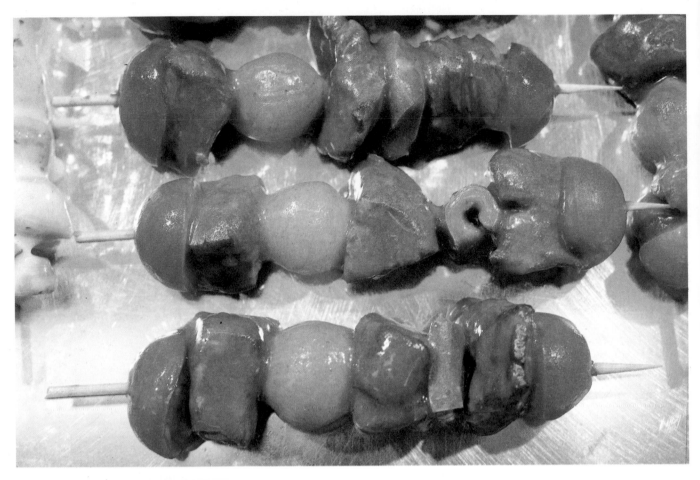

Introduction

These colorful brochettes are made with beef, garnished with vegetables, glazed with a slightly spicy brown chaud-froid flavored with paprika.

They are quite easy to make and the food cost is not high.

Although this brochette is more "ordinary" than the others presented in this chapter, customers

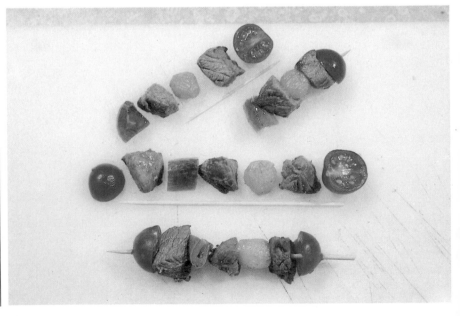

enjoy this classic combination with the spicy hint of the paprika.

This rounds out a selection of cold brochettes. The caterer can include them on buffets, lunch menus or take-out displays.

Equipment

Cutting board, fine-bladed knife, vegetable peeler, paring knife, chef's knife, wooden skewers, large saucepan, three medium saucepans, five mixing bowls, whisk, pastry scraper, fine-meshed conical sieve, colander, sheet pan for draining, cooling rack, tablespoon, skimmer, ladle, measuring cup, parchment paper, pastry brush

Ingredients

For the Main Ingredient

It is recommended to always work with a very tender cut of beef: tenderloin, or strip.

Clarified butter, salt, pepper, paprika.

For the Garnish

Use cherry tomatoes which will hold well on the pick and look attractive.

For the Green Peppers Sauce

45 g (1 1/2 oz) clarified butter
100 g (3 1/2 oz) onions
1 dl (1/2 cup) white wine
1.5 dl (5/8 cup) madeira
1 L (4 cups) reduced stock
Roux (optional)
Salt, pepper, paprika
10-15 g (1/3-1/2 oz) gelatin per litre (per 4 cups)

Procedure

Preparing the Main Ingredient

Trim all tendons and fat from the meat, then cut in small cubes, about 1.5 cm (1/2 in).

This size allows for slight shrinkage during cooking.

Salt and pepper the cubes, then sauté over high heat in hot clarified butter to sear the meat.

Stir the meat with a wooden spatula as it cooks. Do not prick the meat with a fork, as this releases the juices.

It will take just a few minutes to cook the beef to medium rare.

Strogonoff with Paprika Brochettes (continued)

Preparing the sauce

Remove the beef and set aside. Pour off the fat that is left in the pan, add a little clarified butter and return to the heat. Add the chopped onion and cook until soft and light brown.

Deglaze the pan with the white wine and reduce completely. Add the madeira and reduce by half, then add the stock. Let the sauce reduce over a moderate flame, skimming often to remove all impurities that come to the surface so that the sauce is smooth and shiny. Check for seasoning.

If necessary, add a little roux to bind the sauce. The amount of roux needed will depend on the consistency of the stock and the amount of reduction.

Soften the gelatin in cold water and stir into the hot sauce off the heat.

Pour the sauce through a fine-meshed conical sieve and set aside.

Preparing the Garnish

The Green Peppers

Clean and dry the green peppers. With a paring knife, cut around the stem and remove carefully.

Cut in half and trim away any membrane, and remove all seeds.

Cut the peppers into square pieces about the size of the cooked cubes of meat.

Over medium high heat, sauté the peppers in olive oil. Season with a little salt and pepper.

When the peppers have softened slightly, remove and set aside to cool.

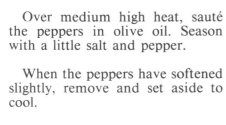

The Cherry Tomatoes

Use firm cherry tomatoes.

Remove the stem and with the point of a paring knife, cut in half.

The Onions

Choose a sauce pan large enough to accommodate all the onions in a single layer so they glaze evenly. Season them with salt, pepper and sugar.

Add a little butter and water to cover halfway.

Cook until all the water has evaporated and the onions are an even golden color.

Cover with a piece of parchment paper cut to the same size as the pan.

Strogonoff with Paprika Brochettes (continued)

Assembling of the Brochettes

Once again, we see that colorful ingredients allow the caterer to create brochettes that are as pleasing to the eye as to the palate.

Be sure to alternate the meat and vegetable garnishes.

Place the ingredients carefully on the skewer so they hold tightly. Keep the brochettes chilled until ready to glaze.

Glazing the Brochettes

Bring the sauce to the right consistency, stirring over crushed ice until slightly thickened. Holding the brochettes over the bowl, brush

them with sauce, return to the refrigerator, then glaze a second time. Chill again until ready to brush on the aspic.

Adding an Aspic Finish

With a soft brush, carefully brush on the aspic.

Presentation

Arrange on plates, platters, or in disposable containers depending on how they are to be served.

Keep chilled until ready to serve to keep them fresh and shiny.

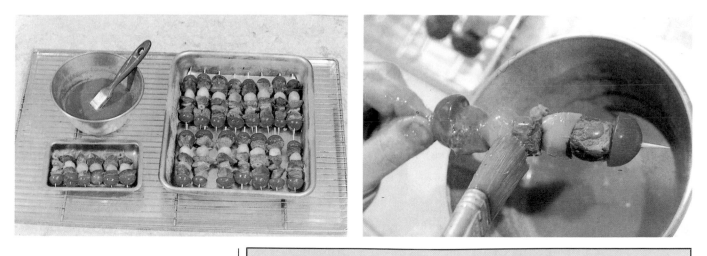

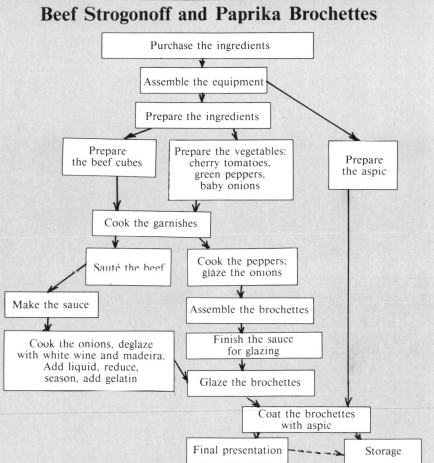

Beef Strogonoff and Paprika Brochettes

```
Purchase the ingredients
        │
        ▼
Assemble the equipment ──────────────┐
        │                             │
        ▼                             │
Prepare the ingredients               │
    │         │                       │
    ▼         ▼                       ▼
Prepare    Prepare the vegetables:  Prepare
the beef   cherry tomatoes,         the aspic
cubes      green peppers,
           baby onions
    │         │
    ▼         ▼
    Cook the garnishes
    │              │
    ▼              ▼
Sauté the beef   Cook the peppers;
    │            glaze the onions
    ▼                 │
Make the sauce        ▼
    │            Assemble the brochettes
    ▼                 │
Cook the onions, deglaze    ▼
with white wine and madeira.  Finish the sauce
Add liquid, reduce,          for glazing
season, add gelatin              │
    │                            ▼
    └──────────► Glaze the brochettes
                      │
                      ▼
              Coat the brochettes
                 with aspic
                      │
                      ▼
              Final presentation ----► Storage
```

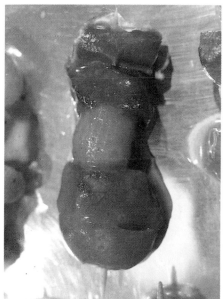

Lamb and Curry Brochettes

Introduction

These lamb brochettes are original and flavorful. The spicy curry sauce is balanced by the sweetness of the fruit garnish consisting of apples, bananas and pineapple.

They are easy and quick to prepare. The meat recommended is leg of lamb, which is expensive but the taste is always appreciated by customers.

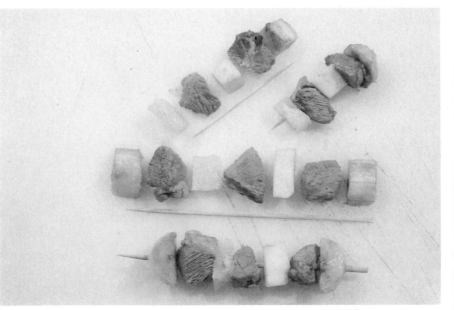

Presentation

For sale in carry out shops, arrange the brochettes on plates for sale by the piece or in disposible containers.

If the brochettes are to be offered on a luncheon menu, arrange them on a plate with a curried rice salad.

For buffets and receptions, they can be arranged on platters or mounted onto a base, such as a pineapple.

Equipment

Cutting board, fine-bladed knife, vegetable peeler, paring knife, chef's knife, wooden skewers, sauté pan with cover, three mixing bowls, fine-meshed conical sieve, colander, small sheet pans for draining, cooling rack, tablespoon, skimmer, whisk

Ingredients

For the Main Ingredients

Always use top quality leg of lamb
Olive oil or clarified butter
Salt, pepper, curry powder

For the Garnish

Choose unblemished fruits to ensure a good-looking product.
Lemons (to rub on bananas and apples)
Apples
Pineapples

For the Sauce

30 g (1 oz) clarified butter
45 g (1 1/2 oz) onions
3 cloves garlic
75 g (2 1/2 oz) carrots
45 g (1 1/2 oz) celery
45 g (1 1/2 oz) leek (white part only)
bouquet garni (thyme, bay leaf, parsley, leek green)
juice of 1/2 lemon
juice of 1 orange
1 L (4 cups) reduced lamb stock
salt, pepper, curry
Roux
10-15 g (1/3-1/2 oz) gelatin per liter (4 cups) sauce

Procedure

Preparing the Main Ingredient

Carefully trim any tendon or fat from the leg of lamb. Cut the meat from the bone and cut it into 2cm (3/8 in) cubes, which allows for some shrinkage during cooking.

Alternatively, purchase the lamb already cut in cubes.

Chill until ready to use.

Preparing of the Garnish

Use firm bananas. Peel them and carefully rub with the cut lemon to keep them from darkening.

With a stainless steel knife, cut them into cubes or slices approximately 1.5 cm (1/2 in) thick. Squeeze a little more lemon juice on them.

If using fresh pineapple, core it, peel it, cut it into cubes about the same size as the bananas and poach them in a light syrup. For canned pineapple, drain well and cut into cubes.

Carefully peel the apples with the vegetable peeler and cut out the stem.

Cut the apple in two, remove the core and rub each half with the lemon.

With a stainless steel knife, cut the apple in cubes the same size as the other fruit, Sprinkle with more lemon juice.

Lamb and Curry Brochettes (continued)
Cooking the Ingredients

Season with a little curry powder while the meat is cooking.

The meat should be cooked medium rare. Drain and set aside to cool until you are ready to assemble the brochettes.

Reserve the pot, as the meat juices in the pan will serve as a base for the curry sauce.

Cooking the Main Ingredient

Choose a pot that will accommodate the meat in a single layer. Salt and pepper the cubes of lamb.

Heat olive oil or clarified butter over high heat, then add the meat, stirring with a wooden spatula to ensure even browning.

Poaching the pineapple

If you are using fresh pineapple, trim, cut into pieces and poach.

Making the Curry Sauce

Discard any fat from the pan used to cook the meat, as this will spoil the sauce.

Add the clarified butter and diced vegetables. Cook over medium heat until soft but not brown.

With the vegetables in the pan, deglaze the pan with the lemon and orange juice and reduce by 1/4, then add the reduced stock and reduce again by 1/2, skimming often to remove all impurities.

Whisk in a little cooked roux to thicken slightly, if necessary. Taste for seasoning. Soften the gelatin leaves or powder in cold water and stir into the hot sauce off the heat.

Pour the sauce through a fine-meshed conical sieve and set aside until you are ready to glaze the brochettes.

Lamb and Curry Brochettes (continued)

Assembly of the Brochettes

Be sure to alternate the cubes of lamb with the garnish on each

skewer to make the brochettes as uniform as possible.

Make sure the cubes of ingredients are firmly on the skewer.

Refrigerate the brochettes until ready to glaze.

Glazing the Brochettes

Stir the sauce over ice to thicken slightly. Brush the sauce over the

brochettes, applying a first coat, then brushing on a second coat to ensure that they are evenly coated, improving appearance and flavor.

Return to the refrigerator until ready to apply the final glaze of aspic.

Adding an Aspic Glaze

With a soft pastry brush, apply a thin coat of aspic to make the brochettes shiny.

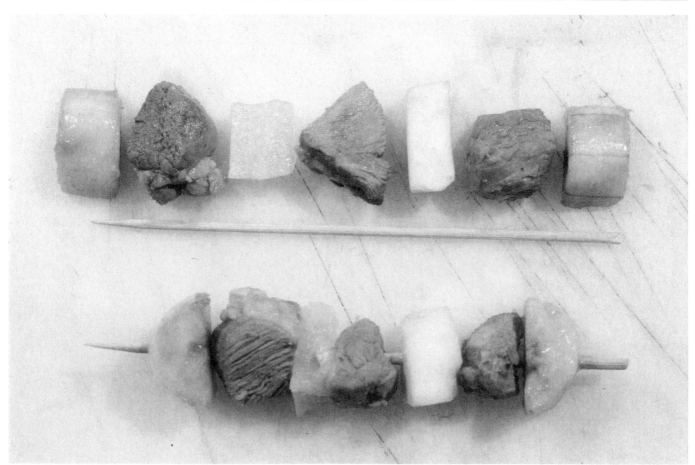

Presentation

Carefully arrange the brochettes in disposable containers, on plates or on platters, depending on how they are to be served.

Keep refrigerated until use.

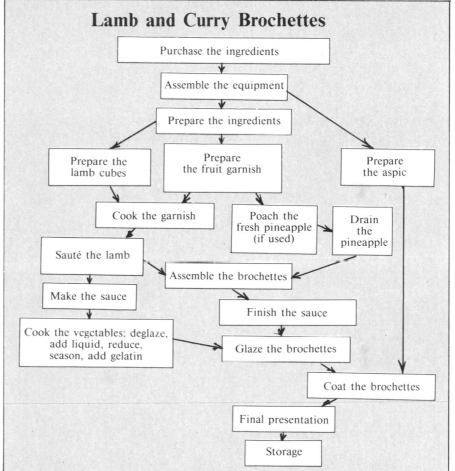

Lamb and Curry Brochettes

Purchase the ingredients
→ Assemble the equipment
→ Prepare the ingredients

Prepare the lamb cubes / Prepare the fruit garnish / Prepare the aspic

Cook the garnish

Poach the fresh pineapple (if used) → Drain the pineapple

Sauté the lamb

Assemble the brochettes

Make the sauce

Finish the sauce

Cook the vegetables; deglaze, add liquid, reduce, season, add gelatin

Glaze the brochettes

Coat the brochettes

Final presentation

Storage

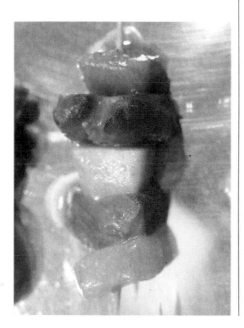

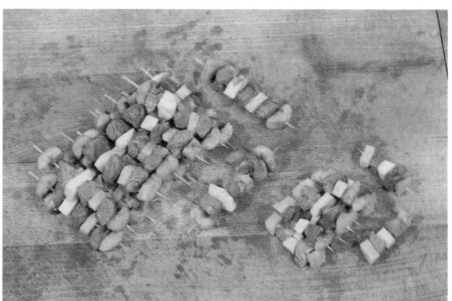

Ham and Pineapple Brochettes

Introduction

These brochettes are easy and quick to prepare and the food cost is low. The pretty colors and the contrast between the sweet fruit and salty ham make these always popular with customers.

Using the right ingredients and the proper techniques yields a sauce that gives a glossy finish and exotic flavor to these delicious brochettes.

Presentation

Arrange the brochettes in disposable containers for sale in a take out shop.

As a light luncheon dish, serve on a plate with a green salad.

On a buffet, arrange the brochettes on platters or attach them to a base such as a pineapple.

If using fresh pineapple, take a serrated knife and cut off the top and bottom. Then stand the pineapple on end and with a thin serrated knife, trim the skin from the sides.

Equipment

Cutting board, fine-bladed knife, cherry pitter, vegetable peeler, paring knife, serrated knife, wooden skewers, one large saucepan, two medium saucepans, five mixing bowls, whisk, pastry scraper, fine-meshed conical sieve, colander, small sheet pans for draining, cooling rack, tablespoon, skimmer, ladle, measuring cup, pastry brush, hand towel

Ingredients

For the Main Ingredient

Always use top quality boiled or baked ham.

For the Garnish

Always use fresh fruit if available, but if not, choose canned fruit packed in light syrup.

Pineapples
Cherries (tart)

For the Sauce

1 dl (1/2 cup) pineapple syrup
8 cl (1/3 cup) wine vinegar
2 dl (3/4 cup) white or red wine -
1 L (4 cups) reduced brown stock
  Roux
  Salt, pepper
10-15 g (1/3-1/2 oz) gelatin per liter (4 cups)

Procedure

Preparing the Main Ingredient

Trim off any fat from the ham.

Cut the ham into thick slices (1.5 cm (1/2 in) and then into cubes.

Preparing the Garnish

The Pineapples

If using canned pineapple, set aside the light syrup for the sauce and drain the slices on a towel. Cut into pieces the same size as the ham.

Remove the small "eyes" with the point of a paring knife. Cut the pineapple in quarters lengthwise and remove the fibrous core. Cut in slices, then in cubes the same size as the ham.

To poach, start the pineapple pieces in a cold simple syrup (1L (4 cups) water to 200 g (1 cup) sugar).

Make the syrup slightly sweeter if the pineapple is very acid. Bring to a simmer and cook long enough to soften.

Remove from the heat and let the fruit cool in the syrup.

The Cherries

Wash the cherries and remove the stems. With the cherry pitter, carefully remove the pits so that the fruit is undamaged and will hold well on the skewer.

If using preserved cherries, remove the stems and make sure there are no pits left.

Poach in red or white wine, starting in cold liquid and letting the fruit cool in the liquid.

223

Ham and Pineapple Brochettes (continued)

Making the Sauce

Place the pineapple syrup in a sauté pan and reduce to a light caramel (it will become bitter if it gets too dark). Add the vinegar and bring to a boil, then pour in the wine. (If fresh cherries were used, use the wine in which they were poached.)

Reduce by 2/3 and stir well to melt all the caramel. Pour in the stock and reduce slightly, skimming often with a small ladle to remove all the impurities to produce a shiny smooth sauce.

Bind the sauce with a little cooked roux if necessary. Taste for seasoning.

Soften the gelatin in cold water. Remove the sauce from the heat and stir in the gelatin until melted.

Pass the sauce through a fine-meshed conical strainer and set aside.

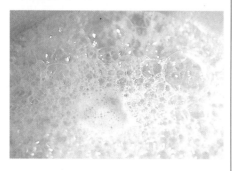

Assembling the Brochettes

Drain the fruits and place them on a towel to dry thoroughly.

Alternate the ham and fruit as shown to create, colorful uniform brochettes. Chill until ready to glaze.

Glazing

Glaze the brochettes with the sauce that has been chilled over ice to thicken to the right consistency to coat. Chill the brochettes to set the first coat, then glaze again.

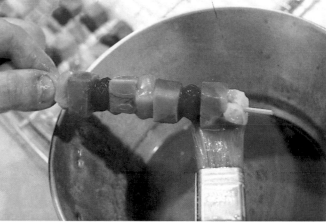

Adding an Aspic Glaze

Once the second layer of sauce has set, apply a final coat of clear meat aspic to protect the brochettes and make them shine. Refrigerate until ready to serve.

Presentation

Arrange on plates, platters, in disposable containers or on a decorative base.

Ham and Pineapple Brochettes

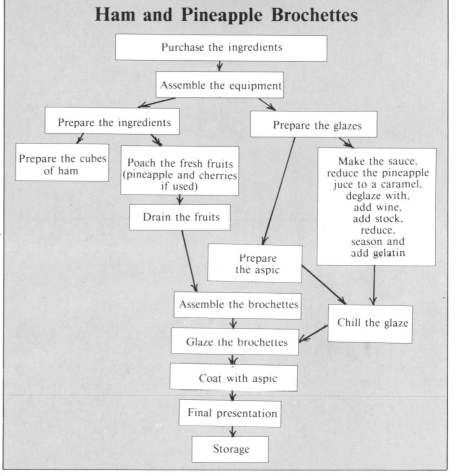

Purchase the ingredients

Assemble the equipment

Prepare the ingredients

Prepare the glazes

Prepare the cubes of ham

Poach the fresh fruits (pineapple and cherries if used)

Make the sauce, reduce the pineapple juce to a caramel, deglaze with, add wine, add stock, reduce, season and add gelatin

Drain the fruits

Prepare the aspic

Assemble the brochettes

Chill the glaze

Glaze the brochettes

Coat with aspic

Final presentation

Storage

Fish and Vegetable Brochettes

Introduction

These are very sophisticated brochettes in which the main ingredients are three varieties of expensive fish, therefore the food cost is relatively high.

These brochettes really dress up a buffet table and are a pleasure to eat as well as to see.

Presentation

For sale in a take-out shop arrange in disposable containers.

As a light luncheon dish, serve on a plate with a green salad.

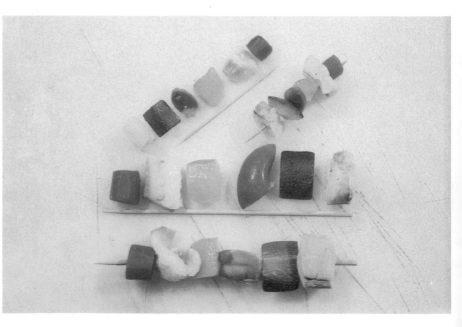

For a buffet, arrange on platters or attach the brochettes to an appropriate base shaped like a fish or shell and perhaps decorated with algae.

Equipment

Cutting board, fine-bladed knife, vegetable peeler, paring knife, wooden skewers, sauté pan, three medium saucepans, four mixing bowls, whisk, pastry scraper, fine-meshed conical sieve, two colanders, sheet pans for draining, cooling rack, tablespoon, skimmer, pastry brush, hand towel

Ingredients

For the Main Ingredient

Use top quality fish: monkfish, sole, scallop coral. If scallop coral is not available, use more of the monkfish and sole or another colorful fish like salmon. If fileting the fish yourself, take extra care so the pieces are neat and attractive.

For the Garnish

Choose bright-colored, unblemished, evenly shaped vegetables which will make it easier to shape uniform pieces: cucumbers, zucchini, carrots.

For the Fish Aspic

Make a fish aspic using clarified fish stock and gelatin. Flavor it with a little saffron.

Procedure

Preparing the Main Ingredients

Use either prepared or whole fish.

If the fish are whole on the bone, skin them neatly, remove the filets of sole and check carefully for any small bones that may be left. Remove them with tweezers without damaging the flesh. Trim and, taking care not to tear them, flatten the filets a little to break the nerves which keeps the sole from curling during cooking.

For the monkfish, remove the gelatinous skin by carefully pulling towards the tail.

Remove the large central bone and trim the filets of all nerves. If available, order fresh colorful scallop coral.

Preparation of the Garnish

Clean, then cut the cucumber in pieces about 2 cm (3/4 in) long. Cut each piece in four and with the paring knife, trim the edges.
Choose a medium zucchini (about 3 cm (1 1/4 in) in diameter).

Clean, cut in 2 cm (3/4 in) pieces then cut in 1/2. Round off the corners with a paring knife. Use carrots with a diameter of about 1.5 cm (1/2 in). Peel and trim the ends, then cut in pieces about 2 cm (3/4 in) long. Rinse and drain.

Cooking the Ingredients

Poaching the Fish

Make a full-flavored fish stock as the flavor of the fish depends on it.

Poach each fish separately. Place in the bottom of a heavy pan. Cover with cold fish stock and bring to a simmer. The time needed to poach each fish will be different, but in general, relatively short due to the small size of the pieces.

Simmer over a low flame so the fish does not overcook and shrink.

The fish is done when it is firm to the touch. It should remain moist, but firm enough to hold securely on the skewer. Drain the poached pieces of fish on a towel and refrigerate.

Cooking the Garnish

Blanch the carrots, cucumbers and zucchini separately as they will cook for different lengths of time.

Bring the salted water to a boil and add the vegetables.

The vegetables are done when they are no longer crunchy, but are still firm. Test this by pricking with the point of a metal skewer.

The zucchini are shown being cooked in an unlined copper bowl, which keeps the water at a rolling boil. (Choose any pot that conducts heat well.) To stop the cooking of all the vegetables, plunge them into ice water.

As soon as they are cool, drain them on a towel and set aside.

Preparing the Aspic

Clarify a full-flavored fish stock to obtain a clear aspic. Add gelatin to the clarified stock. Season with a pinch of saffron which enhances these seafood brochettes and adds a lovely golden color.

Glazing the Brochettes

Stir the aspic over ice to thicken it slightly. Stir gently so that no air bubbles are incorporated which would detract from the appearance.

Brush the chilled brochettes with aspic, return to the refrigerator to set the first layer, then glaze again for a perfect presentation.

Assembling the Brochettes

These are very colorful brochettes. Be sure to alternate the three colors for best results.

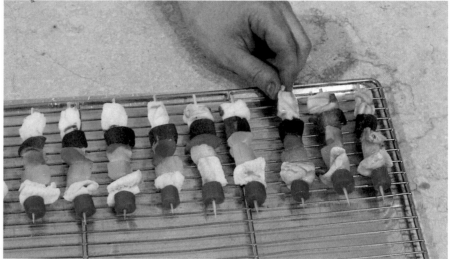

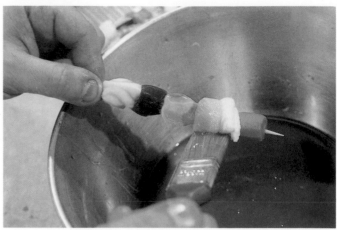

Presentation

These seafood brochettes look stunning when arranged on a fish-shaped platter, or on a bed of algae.

Fish and Vegetable Brochettes

Purchase the ingredients

↓

Assemble the equipment

↓

Prepare the ingredients

↓

Prepare the fish:
bone and trim,
trim the scallop coral

↓

Cut the fish in even pieces
(monkfish and sole)

↓

Poach the fish
in fish stock
and leave to cool
in the liquid

↓

Drain on a
cooling rack

Prepare the vegetables:
peel the cucumbers,
carrots,
wash the zucchini

↓

Cut and trim
the vegetables
evenly. Cook them

Prepare
the saffron
aspic

↓

Finish
the aspic

↓

Assemble the brochettes

↓

Glaze the brochettes

↓

Final presentation

↓

Storage

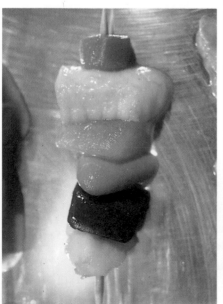

Shellfish Brochettes with Tropical Fruits

Introduction

Shellfish brochettes with tropical fruits are very refreshing and are a lovely pastel color. These brochettes are always extremely successful with customers.

The delicate shellfish combine well with the interesting flavor of the tropical fruits. Aspic perfumed with anise is just the right accent to finish these brochettes.

The techniques involved in making these brochettes are not difficult, but preparation time is relatively long. The shellfish and fruits tend to be expensive, making the food cost of these brochettes quite high.

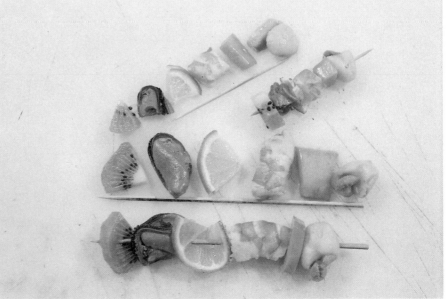

A Variety of Presentations

Like the other brochettes we have seen in this chapter, these can be sold and presented in many different ways. For example, they can be arranged on a plate and accompanied by a refreshing green salad.

For sale in specialty food shops, they are often arranged with other types of brochettes on platters to be sold individually or by the dozen. They can also be presented in small disposable containers accompanied by an appropriate garnish.

At catered receptions, it would be appropriate to attach these seafood brochettes to a styrofoam support in the shape of a shell or a fish.

Equipment

Cutting board, thin-bladed knife, vegetable peeler, paring knife, skewers, 2 pots, 4 mixing bowls, pastry scraper, fine conical strainer, 2 strainers, sheet pan, cooling rack, tablespoon, skimmer, pastry brush, hand towels, serrated knife

Ingredients

For the Main Ingredient

Select top quality mussels which

will be steamed with a mixture of clarified butter, chopped onions and shallots, white wine, pepper and a bouquet garni.

The medium size shrimp are usually purchased already cooked.

The small bay scallops are poached in full-flavored fish stock.

For the Garnish

Select mangoes and kiwis that are ripe but firm so the pieces hold on the skewer.

Fresh dill is used for decoration.

For the Aspic

The aspic to glaze these brochettes is made from fish stock and flavored with anise.

Procedure

Preparation of the Main Ingredients
The Mussels

With a paring knife, scrape away any seaweed and barnacles that may be attached to the mussels. Rinse them well by soaking briefly

in a large basin of cold water, lifting them out into a colander and leaving the sand behind.

Peel and dice the onions and shallots and make a bouquet garni with parsley, thyme, bay leaf, wrapped in a leek leaf and secured with a string.

Cook the onions and shallots in the clarified butter over medium heat until soft but not brown. Add the mussels, bouquet garni and white wine to cover the bottom of the pot. Season with freshly ground pepper. The mussels are naturally salty, so no additional salt is required.

Cover the pot with a tight fitting lid and bring the wine to a boil over a high heat. The mussels cook very quickly. As soon as the shells open, remove the pot from the heat. Mussels that are overcooked are dry and rubbery.

Leave to cool, then carefully detach the mussel from its shell, taking care not to damage it. Remove the dark rim (the beard) from

The Shrimp

Break off the head of the shrimp, then peel away the shell from the tail, taking care to not leave any of the shell attached. Depending on the size of the shrimp, cut in 2 or 3 pieces.

around the edge of the mussel, as it tends to be chewy.

Set the prepared mussels aside and pass the cooking liquid through a fine-meshed conical strainer.

The Bay Scallops

If you purchase the scallops in their shells, open them carefully with a paring knife and detach the scallops. Remove the tough muscle that attaches the scallop to its shell.

Rinse the scallops several times in cold water to remove all the sand and impurities.

Place the scallops in a pot and cover with cold fish stock, then poach gently until the scallop becomes just firm to the touch. Remove with a slotted spoon and drain on a clean hand towel.

The Mangoes

Carefully peel the mango with a sharp knife and remove the large flat pit. Cut the mango in slices, then in uniform cubes about the size of a mussel.

233

The Limes

Cut thin slices of lime using a serrated knife, then cut each slice in half.

If you prefer, the skin of the lime can be removed before cutting in slices.

The Kiwis

Carefully peel the kiwi with a sharp paring knife. Take care not to crush the fragile fruit which tends to be quite juicy.

Cut the kiwi in thick slices (about 1.5 cm (1/2 in)), then cut each slice in quarters.

Assembling the Seafood Brochettes

Skewer the prepared ingredients securely, alternating the seafood and fruits to create colorful brochettes.

Each brochette should be assembled in the same order to insure an attractive presentation.

Be sure to skewer through the center of each ingredient so that they are solidly held on the skewer. Chill thoroughly before glazing.

Glazing the Brochettes

The chilled brochettes are glazed with the aspic made with fish stock and flavored with anise; the aspic has been slightly thickened over ice.

With a soft brush, apply the crystal clear aspic which makes the brochettes shine and keeps them fresh.

Chill to set the first coat of aspic,

then glaze a second time. Refrigerate until ready to serve.

Presenting the Brochettes

Just before serving, decorate with a small sprig of fresh dill or chervil.

Arrange on platters, plates or a decorative base according to how they will be served.

Shellfish and Tropical Fruit Brochettes

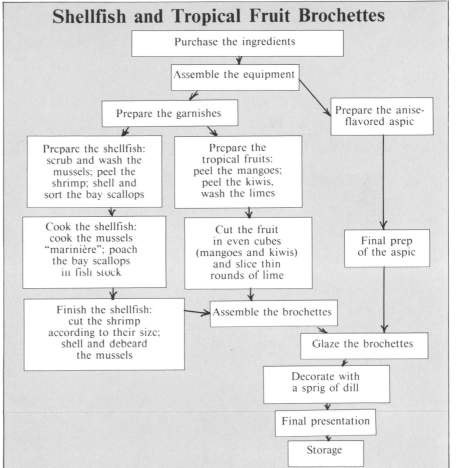

Purchase the ingredients

Assemble the equipment

Prepare the garnishes

Prepare the shellfish: scrub and wash the mussels; peel the shrimp; shell and sort the bay scallops

Prepare the tropical fruits: peel the mangoes; peel the kiwis, wash the limes

Prepare the anise-flavored aspic

Cook the shellfish: cook the mussels "marinière"; poach the bay scallops in fish stock

Cut the fruit in even cubes (mangoes and kiwis) and slice thin rounds of lime

Final prep of the aspic

Finish the shellfish: cut the shrimp according to their size; shell and debeard the mussels

Assemble the brochettes

Glaze the brochettes

Decorate with a sprig of dill

Final presentation

Storage

1. Chicken Glazed with Chaud-froid

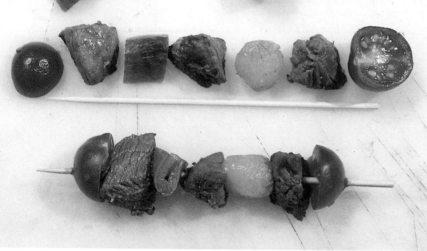

2. Beef Strogonoff

3. Curried Lamb

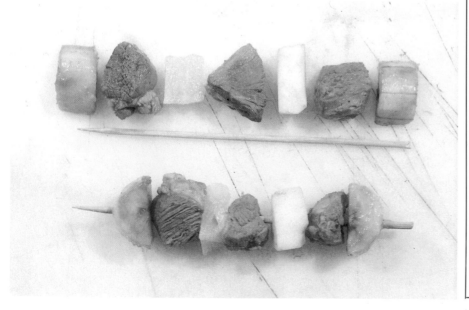

Additional Ideas

Brochettes with Duck Breast and Peaches

Duck and fruit make natural partners. For this brochette, the lean and meaty breast of duck is married with sweet and juicy peaches to make a brochette that is sure to please. A touch of white wine in the sauce enhances the duck and peaches.

Roast the duck breasts in the oven (they are delicious when medium rare). Cool them, remove the skin and cut in large cubes.

Poach the peaches and cut them in cubes about the same size as the duck.

Reduce the poaching liquid to a caramel, deglaze with vinegar, add a little white wine and some duck stock. Reduce, season to taste.

Assemble the brochettes, brush with sauce then with aspic, decorate with fresh currants if in season.

Cheese and Endive Brochettes

These brochettes are a welcome change of pace on a buffet. Choose a swiss cheese with a lot of flavor. Raisins can be used to decorate and enhance the taste.

Cubes of swiss cheese.

Fresh, sturdy leaves of belgian endive cut in pieces about the same size as the cheese.

Assemble, brush on aspic, decorate.

Brochettes with Sweetbreads and Vegetables

The garnish for this brochette is the same as the chicken brochettes in this chapter. The sweetbreads elevate the preparation to new heights and are enhanced with a delicious sauce accented with sherry.

Degorge the sweetbreads under cold running water. Blanch them, starting in cold water and bringing it to a boil for 3 minutes. Season with salt and pepper, coat with flour and cook in oil and butter until cooked through and browned. Cool and cut into cubes.

Glazed carrots, glazed onions, cooked mushrooms.

Deglaze the cooking pan with sherry, add cream and full flavored stock, reduce.

Assemble the brochettes, brush on sauce and aspic.

for Cold Brochettes

Pork and Apricot Brochettes

Dried apricots are suggested for these brochettes as they have the advantage of being available in all seasons. Pineapple can be substituted as well. The light taste of fruit marries well with filet of pork. The sweet and sour note in the sauce adds the just the right touch.

Salt and pepper the filets, tie them with string so that they cook evenly and roast them in the oven. Cool and cut into cubes.

Gently poach the dried apricots. Drain, cool and cut into pieces about the same size as the pork.

Make a caramel with sugar, deglaze with vinegar, add white wine, full flavored stock, reduce, and season to taste.

Assemble the brochettes, brush on sauce and aspic.

Brochettes with Liver and Broccoli

These delicious brochettes are enhanced with a sauce flavored with port. This slightly sweet wine adds just the right balance to the meaty liver.

Cut the liver into cubes, season and sauté in clarified butter.

Choose fresh, vibrant broccoli. Steam it to keep the bright color and to make sure that it does not become too soft. Carefully separate the individual flowerets.

Deglaze the sauté pan with port. Add full flavored stock and cream, reduce.

Assemble the brochettes, and brush with sauce and aspic.

Rabbit Brochettes with Apples and Prunes

This is a fresh tasting brochette that combines the delicate meat of rabbit with fruit. The sauce made with cider brings out the flavor of the apple garnish.

Cut the meat of a boned rabbit into cubes. Season and sauté in clarified butter.

Remove the pits of the prunes. Peel and cut the apple into large dice and sauté in clarified butter.

Deglaze the sauté pan with cider, add full flavored rabbit stock, and reduce.

Assemble the brochettes, brush with sauce and aspic.

4. Ham and Pineapple

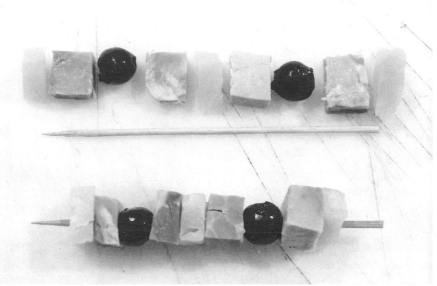

5. Fish and Vegetables

6. Shellfish and Tropical Fruit

Translator's Notes

Because these volumes were originally written for the French audience, some of the ingredients and equipment may need explanation.

Butter is always unsalted, unless otherwise indicated.

Clarified butter is obtained by melting butter, then pouring the pure fat portion off the top, and discarding the milk solids that settle at the bottom and which tend to burn at high temperatures.

Aspic is an important ingredient in catering as it gives a shiny finish to many cold items, as well as keeps the item fresh looking and tasting by sealing out the air. Basic aspic recipes are readily found in reliable cookbooks; top quality powdered aspic is a possible substitute for fresh.

Eggs are always large size (60g/2oz).

" Américaine " sauce is called for in several recipes. The main ingredients include fish stock, tomato, cognac and tarragon. Refer to a reliable source for a recipe.

Drum sieves have many uses in a French kitchen. The large size allows flour to be sifted quickly; meat and vegetable purées are forced through the mesh to obtain smooth mixtures.

Plastic pastry scrapers are an indispensable tool for the French chef, who uses them to scrape bowls clean, transfer mixtures efficiently, keep the work surface clean, as well as to mix pastry doughs.

Hand towels are an essential part of the French chef's equipment. Tucked into the apron, they are an ever-ready pot holder. They are often used to absorb moisture from draining vegetables or other foods; when dampened, they can be used to cover food to prevent drying. When they are in direct contact with food, the hand towels must be perfectly clean.

Sheet pans in France are made from heavy gauge iron that conducts heat evenly. Choose the heaviest sheet pans available.

Measurements are provided in both metric and U.S. units. Most U.S. conversions have been rounded off to the nearest half-unit, except for smaller quantities where accuracy is crucial.

Denis Ruffel:

A Widely-Respected Young Chef

Very early in his career, Denis Ruffel made a name for himself as one of the most talented young chefs of the new generation.

Creative and skilled, meticulous and energetic, empassioned by teaching and always willing to share his knowledge, Ruffel is the ideal author for this series, The Professional Caterer.

After all, who could be more qualified than Denis Ruffel to cover such a field, which includes a wide range of dishes and varied and complex culinary techniques? From the simplest procedure to the most complicated " tricks of the trade " involved in these top-of-the-line recipes, Denis Ruffel offers food professionals a tool that will quickly prove itself indispensable.

For over fifteen years, I have had the pleasure of watching Denis Ruffel's remarkable professional development. Ever since his apprenticeship with Jean Millet, he has had a firm grasp of the fundamental techniques so essential to all top quality work.

Generous with his friends and devoted to his work, he is a paragon of dedication to our profession.

Through working with Denis Ruffel on several seminars, I came to know many of his qualities, including his wealth of knowledge, his modest nature, his friendly disposition, his constant smile and, above all, his outstanding talent for teaching.

His skills, which are equally strong in pastry, catering and cuisine, are limitless and without equal.

The Professional Caterer is the culmination of much hard work and planning, and it stands alone in the field of culinary cookbooks, offering recipes for appetizers to gala buffet fare, and covering the whole range of the catering repertoire.

In these books, Denis Ruffel unites simplicity with perfection. The professional as well as the newcomer to the field can choose from a wide variety of hors d'œuvres, canapés, appetizers, terrines and pâtés and quiches, as well as many other delicious preparations. The recipes are easy to follow, and they are made even clearer by excellent step-by-step photographs.

I would like to express my congratulations and thanks for this marvellous achievment. It is through the work of true professionals like Denis Ruffel--passionate, skilled and dedicated--that our profession will continue to grow.

M. A. Roux

Born in 1950, Denis Ruffel entered the field at the age of fourteen. He received his C.A.P. in Pastry at the Centre Ferrandi in Paris, with Jean Millet as his " maître d'apprentissage ", who very quickly recognized his talents.

Passionate about cooking, Ruffel completed his training by receiving his C.A.P. in Cuisine, and worked, among other places, at La Bourgogne, under Monassier, and L'Archestrate, under Senderens.

Always striving for improvement, Ruffel received the Brevet de Maîtrise de Pâtissier-Confiseur-Glacier, and also studied at the Académie du Vin.

Since the late 1970s, he heads the kitchens of Jean Millet, maintaining the excellent reputation of Maison Millet, especially its prestigious catering department. Despite the heavy workload, Denis Ruffel finds time to participate in many other professional activities:

- Training classes at the Paris Chamber of Commerce
- Administrator for apprenticeship program at the Ecole Nationale de la Pâtisserie d'Yssingeaux
- Chef-instructor at Ecole de Cuisine La Varenne in Paris
- Winner of the Concours du Centenaire de la Saint-Michel
- Member of the Association Internationale des Maîtres Pâtissiers " Relais Dessert "
- Gold-medal winner 1985 of the Confédération Nationale de la Pâtisserie-Confiserie-Glacerie de France
- Honory member of the Confédération National de la Pâtisserie-Confiserie Japonaise
- Winner of the 1985 Culinary Trophy
- Winner of the Confédération Nationale de la Pâtisserie-Confiserie Espagnole (Salon Alimentaria en 1986)

The Professional Caterer is the product of Denis Ruffel's vast range of experience.

First published as *L'Artisan Traiteur* by Editions St-Honoré, Paris, France: copyright © 1987.
English translation copyright © 1990 by Van Nostrand Reinhold for the United States of America and Canada; by CICEM (Compagnie Internationale de Consultation *Education* et *Media*) for the rest of the world.
Van Nostrand Reinhold
115 Fifth Avenue
New York, New York 10003
Macmillan of Canada
Division of Canada Publishing Corporation
164 Commander Boulevard
Agincourt, Ontario MIS 3C7, Canada
ISBN 0-442-00139-8 (vol. 1)

CICEM, 229, rue St-Honoré
75001 PARIS (France)

© CICEM ISBN 2-86871-014-4
Dépôt légal 1er trimestre 1990
Imprimé en France par l'Imprimerie ⓛ Alençonnaise

Library of Congress Cataloging-in-Publication Data

Ruffel, Denis :

Collective title: The professional caterer series / by Denis Ruffel (Bonn in 1950)

Contents:
Vol. 1. Pastry hors d'œuvres, assorted snacks, canapés, centerpieces, hot hors d'œuvres, cold brochette's.
Vol. 2. Individual cold dishes, pates, terrines, galantines, and ballotines, aspics, pizzas, and quiches.
Vol. 3. Croustades, quenelles, souffles, beignets, individual hot dishes, mixed salads, fish in aspic, lobsters, poultry in aspic.
Vol. 4. Meat and Games, Sauces and Bases, Planning, Execution, Display and Decoration for Buffets and Receptions.
1. Quantity cooking. 2. Caterers and catering. I.
Title : The professional caterer series.
TX820.R843 1990 641.5'7--dc20 88-22600
ISBN 0-442-00139-8 (vol. 1)